Jill Kennington Model Years

with
Philippe Garner

Jill Kennington
Model Years

with
Philippe Garner

UNICORN

Foreword

Philippe Garner

Jill's striking image has been known to me since the Sixties – most memorably in high-contrast black and white, her strong features framed by that straight blonde hair, her eyes dramatised with dark make-up. She was one of the most successful models of her generation, the archetype of a fresh, youthful, energised look that defined a decade. As a teenager, I was seduced by her beauty; a mediated vision of Jill Kennington was burnt into my imagination as an ideal of all that seemed alluring – but out of reach.

Now fast forward to 1991. I meet Jill when I am invited to be 'in conversation' with her at the Victoria and Albert Museum; she is an engaging woman; we share our perspectives on the intriguing world of fashion, models, photographers, and magazines. We stay in touch. Jill helps me at different times in my researches into aspects of the Sixties and I regularly encourage her to set down her own memories. She has many stories to tell, but she finds it difficult to get started. Many years elapse before we find a way for Jill to unlock her past. An interview I conduct with her via email for the *Vanity Fair* website in 2011 becomes the template. We initiate an ongoing email exchange in which my questions prompt Jill's stream-of-consciousness responses. The conversational immediacy of her answers is vivid and highly readable. Each answer prompts a further question, creating an unstoppable momentum as the full story unfolds of her life through her modelling years.

The present volume tells Jill's story, both professional and private. She reveals the unexpected personal dramas behind the dynamic persona projected in her published images. Her spirited and frank account, as recorded via our correspondence, gives a very human dimension to the artifice of those glorious photographs that had linked our destinies.

Chapters

The Kennington sisters, Anne, Helen, and Jill, and their cat Pinkie

A rural childhood

precious early memories – life on the farm –
the changing seasons – dressing up

Philippe Garner:
Jill, let's start at the beginning. Do tell me about your family and your early years.

Jill Kennington:
I was born on January 2nd 1943, during the War, in a nursing home in Cleethorpes in Lincolnshire and our first house was a lodge in the hamlet of Riby. My father, John, worked the family farm close by, where my paternal grandparents lived. He was extremely fit, strong, and good-looking. My mother, Rhona, was beautiful, full of hugs and smiles, a real home-maker. Home was cosy in the lodge, with log fires in the evening. I had a sister, Anne, older than me by thirteen months; three years after me came my younger sister, Helen; then, eight years after Helen, in 1954, my brother Johnty was born. He was the most exciting Christmas gift ever. The midwife bustled about all evening before the birth and we were told to go to sleep, stay in our rooms. Early morning on Christmas Day, we heard a baby cry. With stockings and a new baby, all in Mummy and Daddy's bed, what could be better?

I have such vivid memories of childhood. Somehow it was always sunny and we were always outside. When I was about three, my father – we girls adored him – said we were going on a little adventure to Cleethorpes. We arrived at the beach and acquired two donkeys from the old man who gave donkey rides. He was retiring. Daddy gave him a tray of twenty-four eggs, some cream from the farm, and a big sack of potatoes in exchange for the donkeys. They were adorable, one black and one white. Their job at home was to eat nettles and create a clearing in an unkempt part of the garden. Anne and I messed around and rode them and they were a lovely addition to the menagerie of chickens, guinea pigs, Daddy's sheepdogs, and Pinkie, the cat. Grandpa John Kennington, known as Jack, was very scary and strict. He had been a Colonel in the First World War. The big early Georgian farmhouse in which he and Grandma lived was situated at the top of the hill, past the church, with a few cottages round about for the farmhands. This was where we later lived, moving in when we children were still very young, after my grandparents had decided it was too big for them to manage – they moved to a smaller house nearby.

Left: Jill's father, John, with Jill and Anne
Right: Jill's mother, Rhona

Plans always revolved around harvest time. This was a real slice of life on the farm. In those days, the corn was cut and stacked in sheaves. As Anne and I got older, we were allowed to drive the tractors, very slowly so that the men could heave the sheaves on to the trailer, stacking them so cleverly. Teatime was heaven, leaning back against the pyramids of corn still to be forked up, the smell of fresh barley, oats or corn in our nostrils. Mummy was the bearer of Thermos flasks of boiling water and then the tea was made in a pot. Fruitcake was the usual fare and everyone sat together, around a pretty, freshly ironed tablecloth with everything laid out. At the end of the day, after the trailers were well secured, we would ride on top of the corn, back to the farm.

Life on the farm, as I grew up, was wonderful. I helped Daddy as much as I was able, and I was always a happy companion. I loved holding his hand as we went around, collecting eggs, counting sheep, feeding sheep in the winter, moving cattle from one field to another. Lambing time was gorgeous; the ewes were brought in if the weather was horrible, or if Daddy was worried about some of them. We watched births, sometimes deaths. Usually there would be one or two orphans. Occasionally a baby had to be revived in the plate-warming oven of the range in the kitchen. Mummy always seemed to be able to give them back their life. Anne, Helen, and I bottle-fed them.

Once we had settled in, Church Farm, Riby, became a magnet for friends. Anne and I were given two ponies by some good friends whose children had grown out of them. They were called Tatters and Rags. Tatters was a black Welsh mountain pony, very wicked – he definitely taught me to ride. Rags became Anne's; he was a grey cob, the sensible one, and completely reliable. We already had a little black Shetland pony called Heather, who became Fivvy once Helen could talk, and she became Helen's. Although she was a devil to catch, often involving about six people to corner her, once caught she was so placid we could do anything on her - pretend she was a circus pony, stand on her back, crawl under her in games. In the winter, the crew-yard held all the cattle and the last of the shires, called Bess, and our ponies could have the stables.

Our summer holidays were spent in the Lake District, where my other grandmother, on my mother's side, lived, and on the Lincolnshire coast at Huttoft and at Sandilands. The Lake District holidays might involve picnics by Esthwaite, skimming stones, or climbing. We had uncles who would climb anything, and together with Daddy they took us up all the big mountains, the Pikes and Helvellyn. Mummy would drop us off and collect us from an agreed place. We knew all the walks, all the tarns and there were no tourists. Swimming in ice-cold streams, pools, and tarns, crystal-clear waters, was part of being there. Granny saved my life once at Broad Howe – the name of her house – when I was bitten by an adder. It was sunbathing in the greenhouse, where I had gone to collect some tomatoes. I think I put my hand out to stroke it. Of course it bit me. The pain sent me running to the kitchen. Granny said, 'Mercy, darling', reached for a kitchen knife, slit my finger and sucked out the poison, spitting it out of her mouth until she felt it was clean. I was quite poorly for several days. Granny had been a nurse in the First World War. I have a beautiful photograph of her. All this time growing up, there was such a sense of freedom but there were also responsibilities, helping to look after the animals and helping out with domestic chores. School in Louth was very happy. It was too far from home for me to be a day pupil, so Anne and I were weekly boarders. There was one year when we three sisters were all there together.

Auntie Etta and Uncle Tom – he was my father's uncle – were an important part of family life. I have heavenly memories of lazy days in the summer with Auntie Etta at Riby, curled up on the swing seat in the garden, usually with a cat and a guinea pig, gently swinging, singing, and reading a pile of children's books. In the winter, us children would sometimes get dropped off at their house. When the front door was opened, the smell of freshly baked bread or buns drew us in. Uncle Tom would play games with us, using shells from a tin box as our chips. He would put on his beret, at which point he would jabber away in French. I remember lying on the floor, collapsed with giggles.

PG:
You evoke an idyllic image of a truly happy childhood and of endless summers.

JK:
It was certainly happy, though it wasn't always summer. There was an unforgettable winter in 1947. The snows were very harsh and the icy winds made the most enormous drifts. On the road up to Riby crossroads, only the tops of the telegraph poles were visible. Daddy hitched up our Shetland pony, Heather, to a huge sled that he had made and she pulled us up and down the driveway and a short way up the lane. Auntie Mary, Daddy's sister, couldn't come to stay. This was a big disappointment as her Christmas presents to us were London presents and very exciting, usually something to wear and different to our usual clothes.

Every winter, a big box arrived from the Shetlands. It was full of Shetland sweaters and we were allowed to choose three things each. Daddy organised this while Mummy made all our dresses, with smocking on the front. The winter months were creative, with sewing always on the go.

We moved up to the farmhouse when I was six. We children were responsible for taking our own toys. Anne and I used a wheelbarrow and Helen put hers on a sled. The wives of the farm men all came to help us. These women were part of our lives, as they would help in the strawberry fields and with raspberry-picking. Up at Church Farm, something was always going on. There would be jam-making days, fruit-bottling days; and they were a lovely group of very loyal people. There was one farm-hand's wife, Mrs Carter, who never left her house; in fact every time I walked past it, there she was, sitting in the window.

In the attic of the farmhouse was a big trunk. It was full of the most amazing clothes – boas, hats, and shoes. They had belonged to Grandma and she said we could have them for dressing up. I remember spending hours up there with friends who came to play, pretending to be a sophisticated adult. Her shoes were only a little too big. Anne and I sometimes would parade, dressed up, down the drive and past the cottages, with Mrs Carter at the window. Little did I know that dressing up and showing off clothes were to play such an important part in my life.

Teenage years

*a passion for horses – clothes and make-up – first photos –
at college away from home – thunderclouds gather in family life –
a first love – May Balls*

PG:
*Your childhood was a million miles from the world of high fashion, though
I am fascinated to learn of the fun you had dressing up. What came next?*

JK:
The next few years were a flurry of riding like mad, and being blooded
by the hunt, which I hated – literally fox blood, on a fox's pad, was
smeared on both cheeks, and the tradition was that you didn't wash
it off. I found it a gruesome experience, but I was now a member
of the hunt. The enjoyment for me was in the wonderful variety of
landscapes, but I never went near the kill. I went out on Tatters and
had to tie a red ribbon on to his tail, as he had a nasty habit of wanting
to back up to another horse in order to kick it. I was accompanied for
a few years; then I went off by myself. The riding was hair-raising at
times. I was given a beautiful half-Arab for my twelfth birthday, much
taller than Tatters. I would often ride ten miles to spend two days with
my best friend. In the summer, we would camp in one of her father's
fields, cook sausages and green beans for supper, and generally mess
about. I dreamed of horses in those days. I suppose my other passion
was ballet. I dreamed of being a ballet dancer, but I had already been
told by the time I was eleven that I would be too tall.

I remember my parents' bed held special significance. Apart from a
cuddle place, it is where I used to be whenever they were going out
to a ball. Watching Mummy prepare herself at the dressing table
was magic – the finest powder, with a fluffy puff, was dusted on
her shoulders and chest. Compressed powder from a peacock-blue
pearlised compact was caressed over her face; see-through shell-pink
lipstick was carefully applied, giving the effect of naturalness. Out
came the silk stockings that were attached to suspenders. Mummy
pulled on a pretty lace petticoat, being careful to put a chiffon scarf
over her head, which prevented any make-up being spoiled. Then
came the dress; the taffeta rustled when she moved. It was the colour
of petrol and strapless. A brush went through her thick, wavy hair,
gathering it upwards; then she secured it with two hair-combs.

Daddy appeared in a dinner jacket and put on his bow tie, which
seemed so very complicated. They looked gorgeous. Bed was also a

place to watch the ritual of shaving in the morning, the sharpening of the cut-throat on the strop, the shaving brush that lathered the soap in its tub; then, when Daddy was dressed, we helped him with all the buttons on his gaiters, with a buttonhook.

As I got older, I really began to notice grown ups and their clothes and make-up. Magazines rarely came to Riby, but there were movies to see and parties to go to. Clothes were impossible to find, so a dressmaker made our party dresses. What was fun about this was buying the fabric, doing a drawing, and then the dressmaker did her best. As a mid-teenager, the rock-and-roll parties were the best. Our group of friends took to wearing dirndl skirts, little tops, white socks, and shoes as flat as possible.

Then it was time to move schools. Anne was already at Casterton School, which was in a glorious landscape, in the valley of the Lune in the Lake District, and I followed. Life was happy there, but I missed Helen and baby Johnty. Mummy seemed to glow, but a dark cloud started to descend on Daddy. Out of character, he started to get bouts of anger about the smallest thing. As Anne and I were away at school and holidays were full of friends, I suppose we were too busy to know what was happening. Helen was happy to come up to Casterton and she went into the junior school. School life was good academically, great for sports, and inspiring for drama, which I loved.

I had a sweetheart, Martin, at sixteen and was kissed. He was a year older than me and had a car, which was amazing independence. Daddy was strict about my being brought home by midnight and was also very strict about my being properly dressed. There were occasions, though, when the roll-on, almost like a corset, was peeled off leaving nothing to the imagination. How can a girl jive all trussed up? So off it would come in the car. I can only say that my teenage years were such fun, and were spent with some great friends – a few of these friends are still my best friends now.

PG:
I am so interested to hear of your awakening as a teenager, your fascination with your mother's dressing rituals and your own first indications of interest in clothes. But what was troubling your father?

JK:
Mummy said that Daddy was not well. Nothing was properly explained, but there were times when I can only describe the feeling as a thundercloud as Daddy came through the kitchen on the way to his farm office. He would be angry at the pea crop not being harvested

in time, for example, or if lights had been left on by someone in the scullery. I remember being frightened by this force. I kept my head down, but often crept in to cuddle up to my pony in tears. Other times, I remember coming home from school and Daddy had holed up in the top bedroom. It was as if he was someone else. I took lunch up for him and he was a tragic man - such sorrow and guilt for not being his usual self. I felt huge compassion but was unable to figure out how to comfort him, other than with a long hug. He was an ornithologist and had a real passion for birds. Many a day was spent with him, sitting so quietly in the landscape, or amongst the reeds, with mud squishing between my toes, waiting to spot the great crested grebe, to describe just one instance. But now he seemed to have lost even the will to go out. In the next few years, these bouts became worse and he was diagnosed as what is now known as bipolar. We kids wondered if it was catching. He had a psychiatrist, took medication, and, by the time I had turned sixteen, there were sometimes spells in hospital. It was extremely difficult for us all.

But life went on. I did my 'O' levels at school, then went to Cuckfield College of Domestic Science in Sussex. Such a college was regarded as an appropriate 'finishing school' for a girl. Money was a problem and I was given the choice of staying another year at school or going to Cuckfield. This was an extremely easy decision. Anne had been there and it sounded fun, grown-up, and wonderfully close to Brighton. Helen was taken out of boarding school to go to the local grammar school and she then enrolled at art college, which was brilliant for her. Johnty was still at his first school.

My own life thrived. I really grew up, recognised my girl power, and had young men falling for me. Brighton was a buzz. I recall the style-conscious young people there, the little boutiques and cafés where they hung out. It was quite an eye-opener - there was nothing like it in Grimsby, the nearest big town to Riby. At college we were taught about nutrition, how to cook, how to be a young lady, how to get out of a car, deportment, dress-making, and generally, I suppose, how to be an amazing wife! I left after a year, with a First Class diploma.

Then what? At home, I was thrown into interrogations about what to do next. I needed pocket money and worked as a trainee nurse at St Hughes nursing home, the very place where I was born. I absolutely loved working there. It was run by nuns, who were gorgeous women. I was under their wing and spent many happy months there. I also witnessed operations and a death. It brought out my caring side. But I was so restless. I did a course in typing with an elderly lady, but whenever the topic of what I was going to do came up, I kept saying

'No!' I did not want to be a nurse full-time; I did not want to be a secretary; I didn't know what I wanted to do, but it wasn't that. One day, two strangers came to Grimsby. One of them was John, an artist and very bohemian. He played wonderful jazz. He and his friend opened a café. It became the hang-out place for anyone under twenty-five, the first venue for meeting friends and having frothy coffee. We could be there for hours and they played great music. Of course I fell for the artist, and had my first beautiful love affair.

PG:
Tell me more.

JK:
John was a beautiful man, very sensuous, and he was like a hot magnet to me. There was no choice here; the attraction was powerful and he seduced me. For a short while, I held on to the strict rules of upbringing – 'save yourself till marriage'. But I just melted with him and fever heat broke the rules, allowing me to fall into this bliss. Sometimes we would go on a picnic by the lake at Benniworth and he would caress me with summer grass as we listened to the birds. Time stood still. I was in love. I also found him fascinating as he was a painter, philosopher, and musician. I would sit hugging his back as he played free-style jazz; he was so expressive. Did I tell you that Mummy adored him and for years they remained close friends? He also gave such valuable time to Daddy, who was suspicious at first, but the fact is, John was someone he could talk to. There was no age barrier, just a sensitive friend. I knew, though, that I had to continue my life, so the next move felt painful as it wrenched us apart.

PG:
So what followed?

JK:
While I was doing my typing course there was a student, Peter, who I would often go and have tea with after the class. He had the most amazing collection of lead soldiers in a glass cabinet, neatly displaying battle scenes. He always tried to ask me out, but I wasn't having that. One day, my godmother, Aunt Tassie, came to the rescue with an idea. I was certainly driving my parents to despair, always saying 'No!' Aunt Tassie was an avid fan of the Royal Shakespeare Company and drove up to Stratford each season, staying at a beautiful manor house in Moreton-in-Marsh, near Oxford, which had been turned into a small hotel. Run by a battle-axe, it also trained girls in hotel management. All the girls, about ten of them, had come from finishing schools or domestic science colleges. I went for it and stayed for nine months.

It was great fun being with the other girls and being near Oxford. A terrific social life came with it. John visited sometimes, but I was slipping through his fingers. Work was initially a period of house-keeping, followed by bar work and learning about wine, then kitchen, then dining room. We had many regular guests; probably a group of pretty girls had something to do with it. One regular was a BBC television producer from Manchester. He pestered me about going for an interview to be a presenter and he used to pay me far too much attention, which made both me and his wife uncomfortable. I didn't take him up on his proposal as I felt there was an ulterior motive.

One day I was at a friend's cocktail party. Her parents had asked a local photographer to take pictures. After he had done the job, he pestered me, pressing me to come to his studio and saying that he would take some pictures. I did go, as it was very close to the hotel and, to my surprise, I enjoyed the half-hour. This was the first time I had ever sat for a picture. I chose one to give to my parents. Sometimes there would be a letter from home. I was having a great life and in the summer I was asked to some of the May Balls, enchanting and very elegant occasions that turned into revelry that lasted till the early hours. There is nothing like a superb party – with punting at dawn, followed by breakfast and so much laughter, still dressed in ball gowns, shoes off, and with beautiful, dishevelled young men.

I felt that a trip home was necessary for Mummy's sake. Daddy was in hospital. Poor Mummy must have had such a hard time. The love of her life, strong and good-looking, was changing into a sick man. He had undergone shock treatment in hospital, which Mummy explained a little as 'helping' him. It sounded so barbaric and conjured up the worst images. The next day, Anne and I went to visit him. My distress at how he looked is still so clear. This beloved father was disappearing under treatment and medication. It was a shock to see him in bed, hardly knowing us and not able to communicate. He also seemed to change physically and became lethargic and overweight. My little brother Johnty, meanwhile, had turned into a rebel. Mummy had the brainwave to give him a canoe and diving lessons, which he took up with a real passion and which calmed him, but he remained rebellious with authority and at school. Mummy spoilt him to compensate for the lack of fathering, so it was all a bit of a mess. Mummy became a JP, so that and running the local Women's Institute helped her, and she had wonderful, loyal friends, but those were nonetheless difficult, destabilising times for the family.

London beckons

a new decade and a new job – Harrods – flatmates –
spotted by a model agent – picked by Norman Hartnell –
first shoot with John Cowan

PG:
So how did things unfold?

JK:
My relationship with John was now sporadic, though I remained faithful. He became a very good friend to Mummy, someone to talk to, and he would go and play the piano and paint at Riby. My life revolved around old friends in Lincolnshire and a new batch in Oxford and also Cambridge, many of them moving on to London. I was now eighteen and I just knew I had to get to London too. I was spurning all the usual ideas for work. After school, the domestic science college, and the hotel-management training, I needed to find my own path. I had such a free upbringing, a sort of outward-bound childhood. I was fearless and I begged my parents to let me go and stay with my aunt, Mary, my father's sister, who lived in London. I wangled a visit to Aunt Mary and talked to her of my wish to live in the city. Conveniently, meanwhile, I had had a spat with the battle-axe. I said I was not staying for a full year. A plan was starting to take shape.

This was towards the end of 1961. I was happy and excited and in London; it was a huge contrast from life at home in Lincolnshire and there was such a buzz in the air. Aunt Mary was a buyer for Harrods – gloves and handbags – and several times a year she travelled to the collections in Florence and Paris. I went for an interview at Harrods and was taken on. I thought that Harrods might well be my life's work. It was leading up to the Christmas period, so probably late September. It was great clocking in with hundreds of staff, all heading for their lockers, all dressed to code, and me in my first suit. I was put into the cashmere sweaters department – gorgeous sweaters, cardigans, twinsets, etcetera – and I loved helping customers, most of whom were gracious. Cash, notes, cheques, and paperwork went into capsules in a pressurised chute and whizzed down to the basement; the capsules then returned with the receipt – amazing. Lunchtimes were fun – you could meet a friend on the roof café for staff, have a quick sandwich, cup of tea, and a chat. Sometimes, Aunt Mary invited me out to lunch, getting permission for me to take a little longer than usual. She was great for me – elegant, sophisticated, and well-travelled. I know she enjoyed showing me off as her niece. It did become obvious, though, that I needed to find digs. I couldn't come in late without an inquisition, so we both agreed it was time. With her help, I found somewhere in Kensington Gore, very near to her flat and with a good bus route to Knightsbridge. I was waiting for the bus one day and bumped into my friend Juliet. We plotted to try and share a flat.

PG:
Who was Juliet, and did the plot succeed?

JK:
This was Juliet Harmer. I had first met her in Lincolnshire when an old school friend was getting married in the big church in Grimsby. We had kept in touch - the same parties, the same circles. I remember recognising all the usual friends, but across the crowd was a vibrant and very attractive girl I didn't recognise. Funny how it happens, but she gravitated towards me and we totally hit it off. She lived in London, in Kensington. We are still great friends. On that particular day, I was waiting for the bus to take me to Knightsbridge. It was a bright, sunny, and cold morning, with a smell of autumn. I heard a voice calling my name. It was Juliet. We laughed and hugged and planned to meet up that evening. After lots of chit-chat, I told her where I was living and she asked me if I'd like to share a flat, which was affordable, in Egerton Place.

A few days later, we went round and met the hilarious Russian landlady, who wore too much make-up and slightly smudged lipstick. She went wild with rouge, making her look like a Toulouse-Lautrec subject. She walked us up to the top floor. I think the rent was £16 per week. I was so excited. It was gorgeous - three bedrooms, hall, pretty drawing room, kitchen, bathroom. We shared for a few years; already there was a Canadian girl, Ros, and Sarah, who was very beautiful and hardly ever around, except when her mother was in London to visit her. She and her boyfriend, who she later married, lived in trendy Soho. This created the occasional challenge when her mother would ring to speak to Sarah, who wasn't there of course, and I would have to say, 'Sorry, she is out.' Her mother would then call at 8.00am and I would have to say, 'Sorry, you have just missed her.' Sarah was to become my lovely sister-in-law, as her mother became my mother-in-law, but there was a twenty-year gap before we all met up again. It was a lovely flat, which Aunt Mary approved of, and life was a peach.

PG:
You were enjoying London, but tell me how you graduated from selling clothes at Harrods to modelling them.

JK:

A couple of months after Christmas, early in 1962, a big change happened. I was asked to a friend's party at The Savoy. It was being given by her parents. There was an elegant man there who was watching me. Eventually I noticed. It was annoying, but I gave no sign of irritation as he was a friend of the parents. There were cocktails, then dinner and dancing. It was a fun party in a beautiful room. Before the evening was over, the elegant man came up to me and introduced himself as Michael Whittaker, a model agent. He pushed a card into my hand, and insisted that I call him and come and see him at the agency in Brook Street. He said, 'I've been watching you and you have got something special.' He did seem to mean it and was persuasive. The idea came out of the blue; and it bit me. Could I do this? Is he genuine? Better talk to my parents and Aunt Mary. The following day, I rang my aunt to ask her if we could meet, as I needed to talk to her. We arranged to have lunch on the Monday.

PG:

We seem very close to the start of your modelling career. I figure Aunt Mary said okay, but tell me what her reaction was on the Monday? And what were your next steps?

JK:

Monday morning, I took the bus to Knightsbridge, clocked in at Harrods, and chatted with my friends on the way through the corridors up to my cashmere twinsets. I was very excited; I was a girl with a secret. I tried to act normally and got on with my job until my 12.30 lunch date with Aunt Mary. She had sent me a message to collect her in the handbags and gloves section. She was in her office and I had to wait. I studied the kid gloves that came up about three inches above the wrist. On the inside of the wrist was a slit to allow your hand to wriggle through to the fingers, which you then pushed down individually until the fit was snug. There were three small pearl buttons with buttonholes. These gloves were made in Florence and were a part of dressing elegantly. Of course, then there was the handbag, which women carried over the wrist. The smell of expensive leather wafted up. Then suddenly Aunt Mary was in front of me, dressed as usual in a perfectly fitting suit, with a blouse underneath, pearls, and earrings. She looked at me with a stern gaze that reminded me of Grandpa, who would look down at me with one spooky glass eye.

I waited to be invited to talk once we were settled in a sweet, small restaurant at the back of Harrods, where she had taken me before. Dover sole was ordered and the moment arrived. I think Mary was steeling herself for a shock. I told the story of meeting Michael Whittaker. What did she think? There was a long silence while she studied me. Then, to my astonishment, she said, 'He is the best there is for the best shows; we use him at Harrods. You must go and see him.' She explained to me that modelling could be hazardous and that I had good career opportunities at Harrods but that I should think carefully and it was up to me. I felt very much that I was growing up and this was an independent path that I could follow.

I wasted no time and rang from the restaurant for an appointment. Michael said that I could go in the next day at 4.00pm. Aunt Mary cleared the time off. Wow! This felt like an adventure. That evening, I had huge qualms as to what my parents would think. I called home and Mummy was adamant that she should come with me. She drove from Lincolnshire and parked in Brook Street, where I met her. In those days it was so easy – go somewhere; park right outside; no problem. Up we went to his office. Michael Whittaker charmed Mummy, gave her a cup of tea and answered her many questions. It was agreed that I would jump in, not tell my father yet, and work hard to make it a success. I had absolutely no idea what might happen, but I was ready to take the risk.

It was another world in the agency – girls and young men at telephones talking about jobs, clothes, and fittings. There was a buzz. I saw lots of fashion photographs pinned up on the walls. I actually didn't look much like these models. Michael insisted that I come to evening class for the rest of the week, to learn about walking and make-up. He was quite old-school in certain ways, formal in suit and tie, but he certainly understood the business; he was a natural choreographer and could move as gracefully as any model. I kept the day job, put in two hours at the class, and my social plans had to fit around this. The whirl of new things was fun, and I eagerly devoured the 'how to walk' lessons, gliding around the room with a book balanced on my head, followed by how to turn and twirl, how to show the clothes from the wardrobe, and take a jacket off while walking. I spent time sitting in the dressing room doing chignons and make-up. The whole experience was directed towards being able to create a certain elegance. I also had to watch and learn from the others.

Michael was so encouraging. He called me in on the Friday and did two things. First, he made a call to Norman Hartnell, suggesting that he must meet the 'new' girl; and second, he made another call to a photographer called John Cowan. Michael explained to him, 'She must have test shots, darling.' 'You have to meet this bird', he said. 'I think she would be great for you.' Sunday was to be the day for the test shots. Help! This is all happening so fast! My other life was on hold. My mate Juliet was all enthusiasm.

PG:
Norman Hartnell and John Cowan. You were straight in at the deep end. Tell me about these key encounters.

JK:
So I met John – tall, slim, desert boots, skinny stone jeans, open-neck shirt, and vibrant blue eyes. I had been asked to go to his studio in Fulham Road. John was so easy, and I felt okay. We did a few photographs.[1] I felt very green, so he said he wanted to go down by the river and take very natural photographs. He had a blue, slightly battered Land Rover in which we drove to Chiswick. I can't remember what I was wearing but I do remember that I looked fresh-faced with wind-blown hair – walking, standing, turning – and that John was so enthusiastic and that I responded easily to him. He seemed to take lots of pictures. We stopped and had a coffee nearby and I knew I was glowing. John said he would have the results printed during the week. At the beginning of that week I went to the appointment with Norman Hartnell. It was very close to the agency and Michael took me to the couture showrooms. We were met by a slight and dapper gentleman, who introduced himself as the Major. He was very courteous and took me in to meet Mr Hartnell. Here was the Queen's dressmaker, known for his classic, sophisticated creations. I was introduced to a very elegant, beautifully dressed man in a pale grey, faintly pin-striped suit with waistcoat and a small pink rose in his buttonhole, and smelling wonderful. He was very charming. Lots of talk went on about me, even though I was there, but as if I wasn't. I was asked to try on a couple of dresses, then go to meet the dressmakers. Two house models with chignons and piles of make-up were being pinned and fitted. In those days, all the houses had their own models to show clothes to private customers and for house shows; then there were freelance girls for bigger shows.

A big, five-week tour around the British Isles was being planned, to visit the major cities. I remember Mr Hartnell said, 'Darling, you are going to be my mascot.' This meant a bit of special treatment. I was new and they really looked after me. I had to do lots of fittings. There was one dress and jacket that had hundreds of sequins, all sewn by hand by a special seamstress – hours of dedicated work. Then I was to be the bride at the finale of the show and walk down the runway

---

1 Jill is first referenced in Cowan's day-book in February 1962

with Mr Hartnell. He made a big fuss of me. On the tour, I was the youngest; the other girls, as I got to know them, were a mixture of just plain jealous and very haughty; but, thank goodness, two girls were sweet and friendly.

The last night of the tour was celebrated with a hip party given by the Marquess of Bath in the caves on his estate. Called 'The Cave Rave', it was a big bash and I had to wear a witty little suede Tarzan's Jane outfit, appropriate for a sexy cavewoman. Mr Hartnell had this tongue-in-cheek idea as a complete contrast to his collections.

The tour attracted a lot of interest from the local newspapers and most of the time they seemed to ask to photograph me for their articles. Before we left on tour, John had taken some prints to Michael Whittaker. Also, I was booked with him for a two-day shoot for *Honey* magazine, which was fun. This involved basically two girls and two boys dancing around in the studio. Loud music played. Shoes seemed to be a problem, so eventually John asked us to take our shoes off and this worked. The fashion editors were lovely girls and I thoroughly enjoyed the job. This shoot, and the photo shoots on the tour, convinced me that once I got back to London it was photographic work that I wanted to try. It just seemed right. And the diary was starting to fill up with jobs.

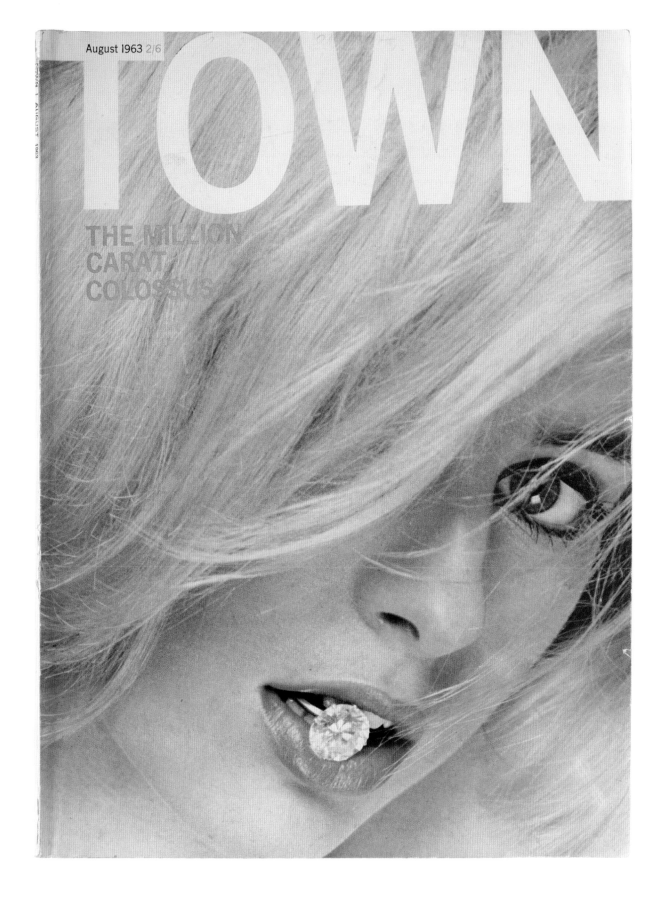

TOWN

THE MILLION
CARAT
COLOSSUS

Jill, by Terence Donovan, *Town*, August 1963

Jill, by John French, for the *Daily Mail*, November 6th 1962

Into the world of modelling

'go-sees' – John French and John Cowan – Fleet Street fashion –
Terence Donovan – Duke and Duchess of Windsor –
a new agent and new opportunities – booked for Queen

PG:
Tell me about those first weeks and months getting established in the
business. What kind of jobs were you doing, and with which photographers?

JK:
The first weeks and months of starting in this extraordinary business
of the world of fashion were a whirlwind. I had done the Hartnell
tour and learnt a lot from watching the other girls, but what I needed
was more practice, finding my way by doing it myself. John's test
shots were great and I remember being surprised that it was me in
the pictures. Michael Whittaker was busy booking me for a London
designer show, to be held at the Courtauld premises in Hanover
Square. This involved a lot of fittings all over London. At least two
fittings per outfit, so there was a blur of different accents, lots of
pins and tape measures, paper and scissors, and endless taxis. I saw
ateliers that were beautiful, such as Frank Usher's, and also the huge
nitty-gritty spaces in the East End and north London, such as Susan
Small's. I was also booked straight off for some photographic work –
that *Honey* job with John Cowan, followed by shoots for newspapers
and weeklies like *Woman's Own* – and in-between I was being sent to
see various photographers, some of whom did a few test shots.

I remember being asked to go to see John French. I was told he was
important. He was very smartly dressed, classic but chic, and wore
huge-framed glasses. There were four models in the dressing room,
doing their make-up. John asked me to come in to the studio, which
was all white. He peered at me under the lights; he inspected me, and
I tried not to feel embarrassed. I remember overhearing him say that
I had a very strong nose. The first job I did with him was for the *Daily
Mail*.[1] There were other girls there; I joined them, and we did our
make-up in a row, each with our own mirror with light bulbs around
it. John asked an associate, Richard Dormer, who had the adjacent
studio, to come and look at my make-up as he was apparently clever
about shading and so on. Once again, I was peered at intensely; then
he shaded my cheeks and extended my eye-line. I felt a bit younger

---

1 November 6th 1962

than the others, and a bit different. On the set, arranging the lighting took ages, with three assistants on hand. When it came to actually shooting the picture, John was to one side and an assistant operated the camera, taking his cue from John, who called out a booming 'Still!' He always did it this way.

A new world was opening up for me – fresh perspectives, new contacts, new friends. I met model Penny Patrick at John French's studio one day. She looked like a dancer, a little like Audrey Hepburn, and we became instant friends. We would criss-cross with one another through our work. We were in New York at the same time once and worked together with photographer Jimmy Moore. Then we would meet in Paris, where she used to stay at the Hôtel du Ministère in the early days for the French collections. That hotel, near the rue du Faubourg Saint-Honoré, became a favourite for me too. The great thing is we are still friends.

Some little jobs where there was no energy, no buzz, I hated and didn't feel comfortable with. I realised very quickly that a good photographer made all the difference. I was booked by John Cowan to do a picture at Billy Smart's circus for the *Daily Mail*. We were five girls, I think. There was a beautiful elephant and the shot was to be of all of us, dolled up with headdresses and sparkly outfits, sitting on the elephant's back. I remember the ringmaster asked if anyone could ride a horse, as there was a lot of silliness going on with some of the girls about being scared. Without thinking, I said I could, and instead of being in the top spot, at the head, I was tail-end Charlie, gripping hard to stop myself from slipping off. It was hilarious.

Next John talked to me about a big meeting with the *Daily Express*. The meeting wasn't in their office but at The Savoy, in the Grill. He had cooked up an idea called 'The Country Girl'. This would involve pictures at Ascot, Henley, the Cambridge May Ball, and so on. Anyway, the *Express* was so impressed that the idea became a series. I loved doing it as it was really lively, involving such scenes as me on horseback riding through the woods,[2] and standing, laughing, on a punt, the morning after the Ball.[3] It was a hit and more bookings came in. I worked with various newspapers, always on location, and I was frequently in and out of Fleet Street for meetings with fashion and picture editors.

---

2 May 28th 1962
3 May 29th 1962

'The Country Girl', by John Cowan, *Daily Express*, May 28th 1962

I fell for John in a big way. A current of electricity went through me when he touched me. We did good photographs. One day, John asked me to come to The Bunch of Grapes, in Brompton Road, to meet a friend of his. It was Terence Donovan. He was large and sort of naughty and a bit flirtatious, with fire in his eyes. We went up to his studio in nearby Yeoman's Row for a while; then we went to have lunch, stuffed peppers, at Luba's Bistro just down the road. There was a lot of banter and laughter. Terry, as he liked to be called, was a one-of-a-kind character, with great warmth and generosity, a very individual take on things, and a sense of humour that belied his underlying seriousness. So I was very happy when he booked me for *The Tatler*.[4]

I made a trip to Paris in 1962 with Michael Whittaker as choreographer to show London fashions. It was a glamorous affair and we were formally introduced to the Duke and Duchess of Windsor, for which we were taught how to curtsey. I cannot forget this couple, and recall vividly how the Duchess reminded me of the Wicked Queen in *Snow White*, while the Duke, I can only say, looked a tragic, broken figure, with huge sadness in his eyes. I did another show in Geneva, also for London designers, and this time managed to miss the plane, arriving only just in time for the rehearsals. This taught me that my private life had to be better managed, with no dancing in clubs and late nights before a job.

Life was great and fizzed, but I realised that I loved the intimacy of photographic work and needed to concentrate on that. The small, tight teams on photo shoots were much more interesting to me than the big show production crews. And this prompted me to find a different agent, whose principal focus was photographic work. I chose Peter Lumley, with a particular 'booker', Jill Rushton, to work with; she, as the job title implies, made all my appointments. This proved, by sheer luck, to be a very good agency for me. From then on, the only shows I agreed to were press shows. The other girls that I got to know included Grace Coddington, Liese Deniz, Marie-Lise Grey, Celia Hammond, Tania Mallet, Jean Shrimpton, Paulene Stone, and Sandra Paul. They had all started modelling before me and were potential competition; so I was glad that my agency was not theirs, and in a short time, work just took off. John and I were regularly being asked to work together - covers for *The Tatler* and then, hurrah, along came *Queen*.

---

4 As it was titled before this was abbreviated to *Tatler*

'The power of positive dressing', by Norman Parkinson
for *Queen*, November 27th 1962

PG:

I want to ask a lot more about John Cowan. But first, tell me about getting onto the pages of Queen.

JK:

I was booked to work for *Queen* magazine with Norman Parkinson. He was so tall and slim and wacky, moustached and dressed in pencil-thin trousers with a flamboyant silk shirt. He was totally charming and easy. The first *Queen* shoot I was involved in with him was a big group story, 'Now learn the Madison with Adam Faith'.[5] I was one of several girls in black cocktail dresses, taking the lead from Adam and learning the steps of this new dance. It was great fun, a very animated shoot that needed a fair amount of space and was shot in the studio of veteran film-star portrait photographer Cornel Lucas, in the Rossetti Studios off the King's Road.

My next opportunity to work with Parks, as he was affectionately known, gave me much more visibility. This was a fashion shoot alternating between me and Celia Hammond, 'The power of positive dressing'.[6] On this occasion, we were in a studio above the magazine's offices in Fetter Lane; people kept popping in, magazine staff and visitors. In one shot, the most striking, I modelled a very beautiful fur coat, with the belt pulled tight and knotted round the waist. I tried it on and Parks said he thought I should arrange it to look as if I was wearing nothing underneath. Such subversion wouldn't have been acceptable at *Vogue*. My hair was done in a hugely elaborate style, involving hairpieces, heavily lacquered and pinned into sculpted shapes like a helmet. It took forever, and meanwhile I did my make-up – Max Factor pan-stick, put on with a damp sponge, translucent powder, a liquid eyeliner, and Max Factor mascara. I used to spit on the block and brush it enough to froth a little, then, raising my eyebrows, I would stroke the lashes upwards. Then I would clamp the eyelash curlers on for a few seconds. I am a girl with straight eyelashes, so I used the curlers quite a lot. A ghastly thought never failed to enter my head – I imagined that the rubber strips had become razor sharp and cut through my eyelashes, which then dropped to the floor. Finally, I did a pale mouth, and I was ready. Parks put on his bejewelled skull-cap before he started shooting. Whenever I worked with him, he always wore this distinctive headgear.

---

5 October 30th 1962
6 November 27th 1962

After this, John and I went to Paris for the collections. We took off in his Land Rover and it felt like a wonderful adventure. We stayed in the Hôtel du Ministère. We had been asked to show the creations of various designers for Iris Ashley of the *Daily Mail*, including Chanel, who I met on her sweeping mirrored staircase. Chanel needed to see me in her suit and give her approval. Iris Ashley deliberately gave people the impression that she was actually Lady Ashley, and it duly worked. She was highly organised. John and I then shot a few pages for *Elle* magazine, which was so refreshing and fun as they were such a lively, young, and enthusiastic team. The whole week was great. Jean Shrimpton and David Bailey were also staying in the hotel, and one evening we went to see American jazz legend Chet Baker playing in a small club - magic! But I have to tell you much more about John.

Jill, by John Cowan, *Queen*, December 4th 1962

An intense partnership

*a dynamic working partnership – stunning images for the daily press –
'The Interpretation of Impact through Energy' – Vidal Sassoon –
Mary Quant and a Mini to match a suit – tensions in the relationship*

PG:
You told me that you fell for John in a big way. What happened?

JK:
I didn't really mean to fall for him, as I had heard, though not from him, that he was married and had children. This went against my ethics, so although there was a huge magnetism, I held off. He swore to me that his marriage was over and I remember my rejection of his advances driving him nuts, to the point of his coming round to my flat and spending the night in the street outside in his Land Rover. With the help of Ros, my flatmate, who adored him and who much later became his secretary and 'all-jobs' girl, I eventually came to understand that he had indeed moved on and was no longer with his wife.

The work was flying in. We had so many jobs together throughout 1962, including many for the newspapers – notably the *Daily Express*, the *Daily Mail*, and the *Daily Mirror* – as well as magazine work. This ensured we were constant collaborators. Then, later in the year, we had a really terrific job that put us together for the first time in the pages of *Queen*. This was a fashion shoot in which I would pose on some of the great statues around London. It became a cover and eight-page feature, 'Monumental ideas about dressing',[1] and proved to be a great demonstration of what we were able to achieve in making striking pictures that were full of energy. I had been to Leonard and he had given me a great haircut, jaw-length but shorter at the back. The editor was less than pleased that I had taken this initiative, but I thought it looked great and, more to the point, it felt very modern.

I shiver to think of those amazing vibes that went between John and me. I was mad about the man and so would agree to these wildly adventurous jobs, having changed in the back of the Land Rover, done my make-up, and had a young hairdresser from the salon check my hair. It is amazing what we achieved; and, although sometimes there was a bit of a crowd, I learned to ignore everything except the wavelength that I was on with John, producing some truly fabulous

---

1 December 4th 1962

work. The *Queen* shoot took us a week. For the cover image, I posed on the statue of Boadicea on the Embankment, by Westminster Bridge. I wore a long, floating dress and was positioned precariously on the shaft between the two horses. Another shot had me perched on the plinth of the Griffin monument, at Temple Bar in Fleet Street, in a black leather coat and boots. For another image I was positioned high in the sky on a cherry-picker in a vaguely nautical outfit with Nelson's Column behind me. I wore furs for a shot on the huge bronze statue of Shackleton in Waterloo Place. For one picture, against the Quadriga on top of the Wellington Arch at Hyde Park Corner, we worked on Sunday to avoid traffic. I was on a platform being raised up when a passing Rolls Royce slowed and a voice shouted, 'Morning! Must be Kennington and Cowan!' followed by laughter. It was Terry Donovan.

PG:
It sounds like you were quickly in stride as a creative team.

JK:
John and I created a stir and, in comparison to other photographers and models, we really had an edge. I was fresh, energetic, and brave; and I was the perfect match to fulfill the wild ideas that emerged from John's imagination. The fact that we were in love only added spice. He understood my bursts of energy and I remember literally having to run round the block, or a field, to burn off the excess. I suppose there was plenty of adrenaline, as we worked at a pretty high intensity. I remember a great picture we did for the *Daily Mail*. I was cast as 'The Executive Girl'.[2] Shot from a low angle, I look as though caught in the down-draught of the helicopter that hovers just behind me, as if waiting to pick me up for some urgent trip. I am holding on to my hat and my face is lit up with this spontaneous expression of excitement. The picture is just so alive.

A couple of weeks later, John had me standing in a bikini on a table in The World's End pub on the King's Road, surrounded by guys playing cards and drinking their beers. This was for a *Daily Mirror* feature, 'What happens when a photographer plans to shoot swimsuits outdoors and it rains?'[3] The shoot was a perfect example of the great ideas and impulsive energy generated when I teamed up with John. Totally necessary was the collaboration of a good fashion editor who, having shown us the outfits, was then able to run with an idea, allowing our creative input. Felicity Green, on the *Daily Mirror*, was

2 March 20th 1963
3 April 3rd 1963

animate Achilles — lean and narrow jacket to a suit of cinnamon and white Glen Check tweed, *opposite*. Flared skirt has a deep ...-pleat in front. Worn over a cinnamon jersey shirt. By Maggi Shepherd, 80 gns. Toast-coloured coney beaver cloche by Peter ...epherd, 19 gns. Both at Woollands. Brown suede boots, 5½ gns. at Anello & Davide. Achilles' accessories by Westmacott in Hyde ...k. To make a Griffin goggle — soft leather teamed with mink. Black calf coat with a mandarin collar and long belt, with a brown ...k beret, *below*. By Yves St. Laurent. Black boots by Gamba, 12 gns. All at Fortnum & Mason. Griffin by C. B. Birch at Temple Bar.

...ORE MONUMENTAL
...RESSING

'Monumental ideas about dressing', by John Cowan,
Queen, December 4th 1962

one such editor with whom we developed many original concepts. For this particular shoot, there was no budget to take us to the South Seas. It was cold, raining, and still wintery in London. We were planning to go to Chiswick, but the filthy weather stopped us. John's Land Rover, which often doubled up as the dressing room, had on board the necessary bikinis, make-up and photographic equipment, as well as myself and the other model, Finola, an assistant, and Felicity as fashion editor. All of us were frustrated that our original destination wasn't viable. In desperation, we pulled over in the King's Road, at World's End, and went into the pub for a think. It occurred to John that, given permission, we could use this wonderful old pub – all wood panels and mirrors – as our location. Whose idea was it for me to stand on the table? I don't remember; however this is what happened. A huge problem to start with was the ogling customers, but these workmen were easily bribed with pints of beer not to look, to carry on talking to each other, and to concentrate on their card game. I remember following my usual plan, focusing only on working for John and not taking notice of anything outside of that. There is a frisson about these pictures, free and abandoned and joyful, in a completely unlikely setting. I'm happy to say, we achieved truly high-voltage pictures.

Another typical John idea was developed for Ernestine Carter, fashion editor of the *Sunday Times*. She gave us a problem to solve with a story on culottes. The challenge was how to show that you can do anything in culottes and not show your knickers! We hatched a plot and Ernestine agreed. John, with the help of a flying club, organised a pilot willing to fly him in circles around me while I hung from a parachute 300 feet up in the air. Of course I had to have some instruction, but basically the chute was tied to the back of the Land Rover, and as it increased in speed, so I went up. It was a wonderful feeling. As John circled in the plane, he shouted 'Be animated!' My face and gestures showed genuine exhilaration. You can see it in the picture. I didn't need that directive. The feature was titled 'Birds in space'.[4] I was of the new wave, not what had been; boundaries had to be broken. For several exhilarating years, we achieved some highly original images, great photographs in their own right that happened to be made for fashion pages. John and I were perfect working partners, united both creatively and in a very exciting affair.

John was now in a studio in Shaftesbury Mews, a little cobbled street between the Cromwell Road and Kensington High Street. The

---

4 June 23rd 1963

'What happens when a photographer plans to shoot swimsuits outdoors and it rains?',
by John Cowan for the *Daily Mirror*, April 3rd 1963

entrance led into a studio converted from a garage, with an office next door and a darkroom. There were big tungsten lights and a roll of background paper, lots of black cables, a big wind machine, a tripod, various cameras, and a couple of stools. That seemed to be it, plus a dressing room off to the side, with the usual mirror with light bulbs all the way round. The fact is, though, that John just loved to work on location; he was energised by the uncertainties and possibilities, and I too responded well to that kind of situation.

PG:
That location work was building you both a great portfolio.

JK:
Yes indeed, and an important and exciting moment that really brought home what we were achieving together was an exhibition of his work that John staged in April 1964. It was titled very appropriately 'The Interpretation of Impact through Energy'. With the help of Kodak, which supported John and also Joe, of Soho darkroom Joe's Basement, he set to it, producing huge prints, 40 by 60 inches, which Joe was equipped to make. Of course they were all black and white, dramatic, high contrast, and very graphic; many captured action; and at least half were of me. The effect was very powerful. I had never seen prints that size.

The exhibition was staged at Gordon's Cameras on Kensington High Street, not far from the Shaftesbury Mews studio. The guest list for the opening was impressive. There were magazine editors and art directors, Fleet Street fashion editors and picture editors, and of course some beautiful girls. I remember Terry Donovan came to support his friend, as did Mary Quant and Alexander Plunkett-Green. Don McCullin was there too. John had invited advertising people and various commercial clients. Tom Wolsey came, on behalf of *Queen*, John Salt for *Tatler*, and my model agent, Peter Lumley. It seemed like all the key players in the fashion and advertising scene, the best art directors, writers, and editors were all there. The power in that room was a huge compliment to John.

My sisters Anne and Helen also came to the opening. It was quite an event. It is all a bit of a blur now, but I remember the compliments flying around. Do you know, I seem to remember wearing a fabulous Delisse silver-thread, knitted shift dress and long Cardin over-the-knee boots. My make-up was all about eyes, smudgy dark, pale lips, Sassoon hair, done then messed up. And of course Vidal Sassoon was there. The party was a great success and a few people stayed behind for sausages and eggs.

PG:

What fascinating encounters with people such as Vidal Sassoon who have come to define the era.

JK:

Vidal was such a breath of fresh air, after the early days of hair rollers and dryers that turned your face red, which I experienced along with every other woman who went to a hair salon. It was wonderful to feel his hands in your hair and on your head, getting to know it and then, with great flair, styling your hair in such a very free manner. He was often on photo shoots and was generous about sending his well-trained boys, if he was busy. Vidal had a unique understanding of cutting hair so that it always fell into shape. You could shake your head or get blown in the wind and it always looked great. I never wanted his ultra-sculptured cut and graphic look, so I was never used for his hair shots, but after an early cut by Leonard, I only went to Vidal. He would be so enthusiastic, his whole body working, sucking in air through his teeth, and just loving what he was doing. He was certainly responsible for the fashionable London look that took hold of the young, spilling out of his Bond Street salon – along with Mary Quant's clothes. They were the team that shaped the times. I had a Mary Quant suit that I really loved, in a deep purple fabric, and when I bought my first car, a Mini, I had it specially sprayed to match the colour of that suit. I have never, I must confess, been that interested in fashion, but I suppose I could hardly be immune to the buzz created by the new young designers who were shaking up the London scene.

Vidal's Bond Street salon was such a trendy place to be that people liked to just drop in. One day, I was there having some waves dried in for a shoot, under the dreaded hair dryer, but upstairs, where it was more private. Someone lifted the visor and said, 'I have always wanted to meet you.' Mortified that it should be in such a circumstance, but giggling, I said hello to the beautiful Terence Stamp. He was surely the most handsome young British actor of his generation; and I will never forget those piercing blue eyes. I used to go to Vidal's parties in his apartment and he was always the same smiling, loving-life Vidal, very charming. Later, when I was in Los Angeles, I went to see him at his sleek house in Beverly Hills. I guess we were friends over many years, though with big gaps. He is memorable to me and I really respect the huge sense of freedom he gave to women.

Mary Quant and Alexander Plunket Greene were friends. They too gave great parties. It didn't seem to matter where you came from, or how you were brought up, the world of fashion and photography was a free mix of all types. It was about being young and using what talent you had. Often, though, we would just get together with Mary and Alexander for a quiet supper in a bistro near Basil Street, or at my favourite, San Lorenzo, soon after it had opened with just a few tables and with Mara cooking.

Plenty was happening for me and I soon found myself in demand as a personality, called on for more than the regular fashion shoots. I recall Radio Caroline wanting me to do an interview. I was invited to the Women of the Year luncheon. Also, I was asked to be the back-up for an appearance in Australia at the Melbourne Cup, in case Jean Shrimpton dropped out, though she made the trip – and caused a considerable stir in that very conservative community with her above-the-knee dress. That was in 1965.

PG:
Jill, you evoke wonderful professional adventures and prompt many new questions about your work as a model, but I would love first to get a fuller sense of John Cowan.

JK:
I know that I have been going round and round, trying to find a way of not answering this question. What was life like, being with John? Well, it was exciting for sure. I had grabbed life by the throat; I was swept up in a current; I was riding the wind. My heart raced a lot of the time. John was very charismatic, and he was fully charged when we worked together. He told me that he loved me. He told me that I was terrific to work with. Strangely, though I am a modest person, when I had my work hat on, I was so strong that nothing would break the spell. In the work situation, I trusted him totally as what might have seemed like reckless ideas were all planned out between us beforehand. Sometimes, the result looked as though we had put ourselves on the edge of danger, but we had studied the problems and I was always happy enough with the plan. I also possessed plenty of common sense. However, on the personal side, he could be unpredictable, sometimes behaving in a way that suggested an underlying lack of confidence, as if he had to prove himself all the time. He seemed to have hang-ups about some old stuff to do with his background.

Being younger by ten years or so, my life was gorgeous and full of friends. I wouldn't wear the bad moods, shrugging them off and going out to supper with a friend. When I first met John, I was not sure where he lived. Then he had a flat in Redcliffe Road, Chelsea, though curiously I didn't really take this into account. I always kept my own flat. But when John took on the wonderful space of Princes Place in Holland Park in 1965, I sort of moved in there.

The Kennington sisters, Jill, Helen, and Anne, by John Cowan,
in front of his Aston Martin, mid-1960s

'What goes on at the old barn?', John Cowan in the Princes Place studio, with model
Stevie Holly, by Phillip Jackson, *Daily Mail*, June 18th 1965

Princes Place became a very buzzing, happening place. For the first time, John had a huge studio, with a small adjoining house, which became a simple and cosy home. We painted everything white, the floors of the house were bare wood, with big, colourful Casa Pupo rugs, one turquoise and another orange. It was functional and unfussy. The studio itself was the full height of the building, really cavernous. It is kind of odd that John should end up with one of the biggest studio spaces in London, as he was not primarily a studio photographer and much preferred shooting on location. That said, it proved a great working environment and had the vibe of creative business going on. The large mezzanine gallery upstairs, overlooking the studio, became a lovely space for work meetings and for entertainment. It made a great sitting room, with the big sofas and a coffee table, and, I'm uncomfortable to say today, on the floor the full-size polar bear skin that John brought back from the trip we made to the Arctic. I remember editors, art directors, designers, and Fleet Street people coming round. Music was always being played; there was a big music system and records, usually a whisky bottle, and big blow-ups on the walls; I guess that was about it. A door led through to the little two-up-two-down house. The kitchen, dressing room, bedroom, and bath-room were upstairs, and the office and another room were downstairs. The little street outside was so quiet, with nothing happening. Until the day John moved there, which brought a great change to the locals' lives. The nearby pub, on the corner of Princedale Road and Pottery Lane, certainly did more business after John moved in.

We were very much alive and John and I fitted so well together. I did feel protected, as if I was in a very safe zone in John's arms. He was tall enough for my head to nestle under his chin; my shoulder fitted under his arm. I was reminded of a glossy fresh conker that, when opened from its shell, would sometimes be split in two parts, each its own, but together making a perfect whole.

PG:
You were in love with John, but it seems things were not always easy.

JK:
You are right; things were far from straightforward. So we come back to John's personality. I do find it extremely difficult to talk about him as a man. He was so complex. When we worked, he was at his best, with problems to solve and with my determination to help create a great photograph. But, when he wasn't working, he could be difficult and moody. There were times when he drank too much and was no longer the upbeat, fun guy who was so charismatic, but became broody and dark. He had things to worry about, for sure. He had three

children and his wife to support and he was often broke. I didn't get involved with his financial affairs after bailing him out a few times and not being paid back. I was also very resistant to his pressure to join a model agency that he was setting up. Obviously, as we had rapidly built up such a strong profile in the business, he wanted me on board; but I was wary. I knew John well enough to suspect it would not be a smooth ride from a practical, business perspective. And of course I resisted as I did not want to be owned or controlled by John and I definitely needed to be free to work with other wonderful photographers.

I always felt that John carried a serious chip on his shoulder. His whole persona was constructed around an image he projected of himself as a very English kind of gentleman adventurer. But I suspect this was a way of denying the realities of his background and there was a constant tension in the fundamental conflict between the image and the reality. He preferred to create a veil of mystery over his family. I really don't understand why this was an issue for him, as we were in such a great new era in which there was a breaking down of class barriers and opportunities were open to talented people from all backgrounds for the first time. Indeed, within his chosen career as a photographer, a working-class background had become a highly fashionable sign of authenticity. So if you had talent, that was what really counted. But it was an issue for John, and it explains the contrast of bluster and insecurity that characterised him. John enjoyed a good friendship with Terry Donovan; he was flattered by the esteem in which he was held by Lord Lichfield. A photo Lichfield did of me in 1964 - in leather coat and driving goggles, leaning against a Cooper Formula Junior, shot from a first-floor window of his Belgravia mews studio - surely, dare I say, owes a debt to John. But he kept a certain distance from most of the photographers who made up that new scene.

Perhaps surprisingly, considering how close John and I were, I only once met his mother. We were working on the coast near Margate. It may have been when we made pictures of me naked on the white horse for *Queen*.[5] Anyway, when the job was done, he said, 'My mother lives near here. Let's call in.' When we visited her, I saw that she lived very modestly. I remember being taken aback at the cool peck on the cheek and the lack of any sign of affection between the two of them. What a difference between our relationships with our respective mothers. I felt so lucky that I was loved so much. A huge hug would

---

5 'An olde English love affair', May 19th 1965

Jill, by Lichfield, September 1964

be my welcome. So there were signs of damage and it felt sad. His mother appeared sad. There wasn't a lot I could do about it and John wouldn't talk about it. His mother had remarried and I realise that I knew absolutely nothing about his father.

What was lacking there was made up for with my family, who just accepted him as he was. My sisters thought he was great; my little brother hero-worshipped him; and my mother welcomed him, although she worried about whether or not he would marry me. My father was more suspicious. But we were always welcome at Church Farm, Riby, and often there were parties to go to, usually a friend's 21st or wedding. I remember that John was a magnet to the girls, but most of the boys were guarded and some were clearly jealous that he, rather than they, had my attention. He once did an appalling stunt. In a friend's beautiful home - all parquet flooring and antique furniture - he decided to show an adoring, giggling crowd how to flame-throw by taking a swig of lighter fluid, and then spurting it out of his mouth while lighting it. Aaaggghhh! Typical John bravura. Thank God there wasn't a serious accident. My friends accepted him and we had great fun. John was also very kind and very protective of me when I had a terrible car crash in the winter of 1964-5. He was wonderful. He was there for me after that trauma and when I was terrified that the facial injuries I had suffered would mean the end of my career. Mercifully, broken bones and skin healed and I was able to get back to work.

PG:
You evoke a forceful personality. How did you juggle his tendency to be controlling and your desire to preserve your professional independence?

JK:
John could be moody when I didn't agree to doing certain jobs with him. I was freelance and very determined to remain so. I wanted to work with other great photographers when the opportunities arose. It felt so much better for me as a person to explore my potential by working with different talents. He got upset and drank too much whisky when I did a fabulous trip to Kenya with American photographer, writer, and adventurer Peter Beard. John and I had been asked, after I confirmed the Kenya job, to do a trip for American *Vogue*. He became very insistent that I should pull out of the Kenya trip in order to work with him for *Vogue*. He wouldn't let go, but neither would I. Sometimes his finances went awry and I paid off the bailiffs more than once before eventually refusing to settle his debts. Some fashion editors loved John and others hated him. He could be both a rogue and a flirt, and deep down I questioned whether or not I really trusted him.

By now John had splashed out and bought an Aston Martin – most likely inspired by James Bond in *Goldfinger*. He still had the Land Rover but the Aston was a beauty, kitted out with the first car radio that I had encountered. So John appeared full of panache, giving the impression that life was successful. I adored John, but he wouldn't totally commit and eventually my suspicions of his flirtation with someone else proved justified.

'Young Idea: Prototype '63', by Terence Donovan, British *Vogue*, June 1963

Branching out

Vogue and 'Young Idea' – to Cyprus for the Weekend Telegraph *–*
Vogue *covers with David Bailey –*
Guy Bourdin and Jeanloup Sieff – Clare Rendlesham and Queen

PG:
*You became very closely associated with John, but you still worked with
other photographers.*

JK:
Yes, John and I were a couple and we regularly worked together, but,
as I've said before, I always worked with other photographers too. I
realised this was important for my career and for my own sense of
fulfillment. There were constant offers of work. My agent used to say
that I could keep the agency going on what I turned down. I knew by
now that I had something special and needed to keep keen. Other parts
of my emotional make-up came out with different photographers.
The pictures I did with John were important in establishing my
reputation, but I wanted to explore other ways of working.

I was delighted early in 1963 to get my first bookings for *Vogue*. These
were for the 'Young Idea' pages with fashion editor Clare Rendlesham.
She tried me out on a rapid succession of studio shoots, first with
Terry Donovan,[1] then with Gene Vernier,[2] then with Peter Carapetian.[3]
These went well enough, though did not match the imaginative
location work I was doing with John. But it was a welcome start in
Vogue and before long Clare cast me, along with Grace Coddington,
for a location shoot in and around Bath with the delightful Peter Rand,
who knew how to create a relaxed mood that led to stylish, seemingly
effortless pictures.[4] Peter did a great headshot of me in the *Vogue*
studio around this time – simple and arresting, just my head against
blackness – but I'm not sure it ever got published. The Bath job was
fun, but even more exciting was a second feature for that same issue
with Terry Donovan, in which I was named – 'Jill Kennington, model
for a year and 20, is Young Idea's 1963 quintessence.'[5] Wow! I was so
thrilled to get that attention in *Vogue*; and I loved the lead photograph
– a full-face portrait, quite tightly cropped, very confrontational.

---

1 'Young Idea: The '30s look / The '40s look', March 1st 1963
2 'Young Idea's separable separates', April 1st 1963
3 'Young Idea: The Short and the Tall / The Long and the Short', April 15th 1963
4 'The beauties of Bath', June 1963
5 'Young Idea: Prototype '63', June 1963

My make-up suggests a slightly metallic sheen. Having worked for *Tatler* and made my mark in *Queen*, I was now featured in *Vogue*. The picture was very different in feeling from the more classic look of the beauties who graced the *Vogue* pages. It was very present and sort of 'This is me, the new kid on the block!' I loved working with Terry, though I remember being a bit scared the first time. He and his assistant talked gobbledygook with lots of cockney slang thrown in for good measure; they had a code, so they could talk about you in front of you. I hadn't a clue what they were saying. Terry was a technical whizz and at the same time had an ability to create a kind of intimacy when getting the shot. His assistant Clive would leap in with a little glass full of glycerine and a small brush, taking time to dab my lips to make them shine while bantering away, and the result was great. Terry was such an engaging character and always great company. We worked on some good jobs – a big BP ad, shots for *Tatler*, *Vogue*, *Queen*, and the *Weekend Telegraph*. We went on a wonderful trip to Cyprus for the *Weekend Telegraph* in 1966 to shoot summer clothes and swimwear.[6] The fashion editor was Cherry Twiss. She was an attractive young woman and quite feisty, happy to boss people around to achieve what she wanted, much like a Head Girl. She had worked as a model before getting jobs with *Vogue* and then *Queen*, so she knew the business inside out. She had quite an appetite for adventure and conceived some great location shoots when she joined the *Telegraph*. These would run over several spreads and often the cover as well, as was the case with the Cyprus shoot, in which I am stretched out at the water's edge in a silver bikini. Cherry was bright; she had class, and certainly a great instinct for talent and possibilities, shrewdly putting together the right photographer, model, and location. We worked with William Klein in Paris and Saul Leiter in Scotland, as well as with Terry in Cyprus. The magazine was published in a good large format which did justice to the photographs. It was always interesting and fun to work with Cherry, a kindred spirit who embraced every aspect of an experience, including culture, food, and conversation.

PG:
Thinking of the prominent London photographers, did you work with David Bailey?

JK:
Yes. On several occasions. I remember there was always music in the studio at *Vogue* when Bailey was at work, so the atmosphere was welcoming. He was small and appeared naughty; he seemed self-

---

6 'Aphrodite's Island', January 6th 1967

WHITEWASHED *church above, built on the rocks of Kyrenia, is typical of Greek Cypriot architecture. Silk pyjamas by Ken Scott, from Patsy B. Boutique, 6 Upper Grosvenor Street, London W1. Silver and turquoise bracelet, 33 gns, with matching ring, 19 gns, designed and made by Rod Edwards, from the Craft Gallery, 178 Kensington Church Street, W8. Bloodstone and amethyst rings, in silver, 7 gns and 12 gns respectively, from a collection of jewellery by Barbara Cartlidge at the Craft Gallery*

18

'Aphrodite's Island', by Terence Donovan, *Weekend Telegraph*, January 6th 1967

assured about work and would argue with fashion editors if necessary to impose his ideas. I remember that during my first job with him there was a young photographer busily taking pictures of us at work. That was Terry O'Neill. So I felt I was truly on set. People regularly turned up to chat with Bailey and I remember Mick Jagger coming in, and on another occasion Catherine Deneuve, who he married in the summer of 1965. Bailey didn't seem to mind an audience; on the contrary, he loved the attention. I did a couple of *Vogue* covers with him – one in a hat with colourful spots and with bright red lipstick and red nails,[7] and another with three of us in sculpted 'Op Art' hats.[8] The two other girls were Sue Murray, who was so sweet, and Moyra Swan. I never felt like a cover girl, as most covers were tightly styled studio shots and I preferred jobs that gave me more opportunity to express myself, although, over the years, I did many covers, for *Elle*, *Queen*, and various Italian magazines. Usually, these were taken in the context of a shoot, as with my 1974 French *Vogue* trip to Sudan with Gian Paolo Barbieri.

I remember doing a cool picnic photograph with Bailey for *Vogue*[9] down at Camber Sands, this time in the dunes. It was the only time I worked on location with him. We also did a big full-face over a double-page spread, half made up and the other half natural;[10] but there were not so many jobs with Bailey. I seemed to click more with other photographers; and I did disappear from London for years that I spent abroad. Hats off to Bailey though; he was always there and still is, which is phenomenal.

PG:
And what about some of the top Paris-based photographers?

JK:
One now-legendary French photographer I worked with was Guy Bourdin, though I first met him in London, in the dressing rooms of the *Vogue* studios. I was one of several models booked for the shoot, though we each posed individually.[11] I found myself sitting in front of the bank of lights, no doubt wondering what the day held with this new French photographer. There were mirrors in a line down one side of the room for us models, each with light bulbs going right round,

_____

7 August 1965
8 September 15th 1965
9 'Picnics', July 1965
10 'The face makers', September 1st 1966
11 'This summer's fashion certainties', April 1st 1966

VOGUE

SEPTEMBER 15 1965 3/-

positive looks in
black and white and
YOU add the colour*
first Shrimpton designs*
racy new furs*

Jill, with Sue Murray and Moyra Swan, by David Bailey,
British *Vogue*, September 15th 1965

and daylight windows at the end. In addition to a comfortable chair, the opposite wall was taken up by a line of clothes rails and a few light dressing gowns. I always got out of my own clothes and put on a gown before starting make-up, so that was how I looked when Guy came in, with an assistant, to introduce himself to us. He wore glasses, was not very tall, and had an aura of moody thoughtfulness. Guy said he wanted to show me some pictures. We went to the window and he pulled out of his jacket pocket a handful of colour transparencies. They were of windows, seen from the inside, and I remember one or two had white doves flying, or sitting on the sill. These were pictures of his paintings. This made a big impression on me. It was his oblique way of sharing something about himself and the inner world of his imagination. I remember seeing photographs of his a few years later that incorporated exactly that subject.

He did take some amazing photographs for French *Vogue* and then of course there were the now-famous ad campaigns for Charles Jourdan. I worked with him in Paris a few times; one shoot was for *Elle*, taken on wasteland – a new development site on the outskirts of Paris with unfinished tower blocks. Another time we worked in his studio. I remember that his mood was troubled and dark; he didn't seem to know what he wanted to do, but perhaps, more likely, that was just an act to create a certain tension. It was a strange experience for me.

I have this memory of him wanting very red lipstick, which was a look he became known for later when photographing very young girls – pale skin, intensely red lipstick, sometimes looking rather deathly but to amazing effect. The last job we did together was before I left for Rome. That was the last time that I saw him, so I guess it must have been towards the very end of the Sixties.

PG:
Jill, which other French photographers made an impression on you?

JK:
I was thrilled to work with the gorgeous Jeanloup Sieff on a cover shot for *Queen*.[12] He was a beautiful Frenchman with a rare quietness, a stillness. And we did a location feature for *Queen* called 'Peasant Black'.[13] These have remained some of my favourite photographs. Shooting in black and white for the feature, Sieff, who was a master of tone, captured a certain mood, mysterious and melancholic. The

---

12   December 2nd 1964
13   December 16th 1964

PEASANT BLACK

Black's back, from top to toe. Black's backed by fashion, not just for evenings but ultra-chic for the country, after all that camouflaging camel and vague beige. Very strong. Very earthy. Very fundamental. Black livens textures – fur, chenille, loosely woven tweeds, lacy stockings. For peasant black, a homespun face. Minimum make-up, small un-back-combed heads. All very simple, stirring something in your dark primaeval depths. Opposite: black quilted coat in matt rayon silk, straight and unaffected, double-breasted with tailored revers and tie belt. By Armand Fouks, £45 at the House of Auberne, 75 New Bond Street W1. Black crochet hat by James Wedge, 7½ gns at Liberty, Regent Street W1. Below: braided cloche in finely stitched black silk, with a chic jet whirligig in front. By Graham Smith. About 22 gns at Fortnum & Mason, Piccadilly

'Peasant Black', by Jeanloup Sieff, *Queen*, December 16th 1964

fashion editor was Clare Rendlesham, who I had already worked with on *Vogue*. We seemed to work well together and when she moved to the fashion pages of *Queen*, we did some great jobs. We stayed at Clare's cottage in Wiltshire, using the Downs and her garden as a setting. It was a five-day job and on one of the days we were joined by another girl – Pattie Boyd. Although I knew Pattie, I had only once been photographed with her. She was the perfect 'dolly bird' and had started dating George Harrison. I remember I took her to the station afterwards and we met a stray pig in the lane. Being a farmer's daughter, I knew I had to put it back in the field, rather a task as it was a huge Saddleback. All the time, Pattie was saying, 'Hurry up, I've got to catch the train – I mustn't be late for George!'

Another lovely job with Jeanloup was for the *Weekend Telegraph* magazine.[14] The two-model shoot was down in Rye and planned for very early morning. We stayed the night at The Mermaid Inn and had a cosy supper by a log fire. Jeanloup wanted to be on the sands soon after dawn, to take advantage of that gorgeous raking light. I remember feeling so glamorous for one shot in particular, leaning against an Alfa Romeo in an ostrich-trimmed pink silk chiffon gown. The photographs came together easily; they were styled very simply, with hardly any make-up, just blowing hair, though they must have taken some organising by the magazine team as they involved showing off several beautiful cars, previewing the Motor Show. In another shot, I sat on the bonnet of a white Ford Mustang, my face partially hidden by a white horse. I really enjoyed the editorial freedom of those magazines that were not purely fashion magazines. They attracted independent-minded fashion editors like Cherry Twiss on the *Weekend Telegraph* and Clare Rendlesham on *Queen*.

PG:
You featured prominently in Queen, *didn't you?*

JK:
That was such a terrific magazine and one that I got to know well. I loved working with *Queen* ever since that first shoot with Parkinson. I did some great spreads with Helmut Newton, Peter Beard, John Cowan, and David Montgomery, who worked quite a lot for the magazine. David had arrived from New York in the early Sixties, and he was very, very good. He was laid back, with his drawl and unhurried way. He always set his own pace. The job was eventually finished and the pictures achieved, but you never knew how long that might take.

---

14 'Cars and fashion 1964', October 9th 1964

He had a big studio in Edith Grove, Chelsea, all black with cool music playing, a good working atmosphere.

Clare Rendlesham had such a way with clothes and she had a great instinct about photographers. Many people thought she was a nightmare, but we clicked and all the shoots I did with her were terrific. These included a number of shoots for which Clare teamed me up with David Montgomery. One shoot we did with David was called 'Manely Romantic'.[15] Clare's idea was to emphasise my hair, which was styled into big shapes, hence the play of words for the feature title. The thing about the team at *Queen* was that they really gave people a chance to be creative, and they were bold and confident enough to take risks. They gave many photographers a first chance, local as well as foreign, including budding French and American photographers, before they were used by *Vogue*; and they were young and refreshing. The art department and the directors sometimes had editorial-meeting battles on Monday mornings that became legendary. But the creative team had the confidence to fight to defend their ideas, and this was essential as they recognised the pulse of what was happening in London.

---

15 'Manely Romantic', September 9th 1964

To New York

the legendary Eileen Ford agency – working with Richard Avedon,
Bob Richardson, Saul Leiter, Bert Stern, and William Klein

PG:
Jill, you were enjoying huge success in London, but New York also beckoned around this time, didn't it?

JK:
Yes, of course, and that was a great adventure. This was way before jet travel became the everyday thing it is today. I made my first trip to New York, with John, in 1963. We were back again in April 1964, very soon after the opening of John's London exhibition. The city was such a strong jolt to one's senses. It was so vibrant and so diverse. It felt like a country on its own; it had its own personality, its own dynamic. It was just so exciting to be there; New York gave me energy, but if I stayed too long it sapped all my reserves. I needed a work permit and this was organised through the Eileen Ford model agency. They quickly got me started, making connections and getting jobs. Some of the studio spaces were huge, often in big industrial buildings, with great rattling lifts for moving cargo. Once up in these loft spaces, full of light, with music playing very loudly, you were in another world, but this was my world and I felt totally at home.

PG:
Eileen Ford is a legend. What were your impressions of her?

JK:
When I think of Eileen, I also think of her husband Jerry. They were both a couple and business partners, laughing a lot, arguing a lot, and working brilliantly together. Eileen had guts and pizzazz while Jerry had charm and was very kind, a good family man. When I first arrived in New York with John, they were expecting us and became the first port of call. The first night on that first trip was spent at their house. They were so welcoming and it was a chance for us to get to know each other and to meet their children – Jamie, Billy, Katie, and Lacey – before moving in to a pre-arranged apartment. Eileen had huge expectations that, as an invited cool English model, I was going to do some good work and make her money. The agency had a buzz and it felt very professional, which it was. I was introduced to all the bookers, and then Eileen, with a keen eye, said, 'Well, we will have to fix your nose.' All the girls had petite noses and mine had character.

It had been broken once, so I was not perfect. Well, I took umbrage at this; I was doing very well, thank you, with my own face. She soon discovered that she was the only person to make this comment.

Work was fun and the agency was great, but Eileen didn't like it if I said I didn't want to do something, telling me that her top girls never refused anything. She soon discovered that I could get class jobs and I was happy with that, but I didn't want to be just another model in the filing cabinet of blondes. I met girls who trailed from studio to studio, made-up and ready to do just one outfit in ten minutes, then on to the next job, actually ploughing through many separate jobs in a day. This was a different way of working compared to creating a spread, or concentrating on a good advertising job, which might take most of the day for just one image. I was in New York and loving the pace and the buzz. Eileen and Jerry were constantly inviting me to dinners with clients. Hmm … I was not too keen. But there were also invitations for weekends at their lovely house in Quogue, Long Island. There were usually a few other people staying and the weekends were all about the beach, cooking, barbecuing, tennis with Jerry, shoes off for Eileen; as for me, Katie, and Lacey, we were doing gymnastic displays in the hall. Lots of laughter comes to mind, and driving in the big American limo with the radio playing. They were very kind to me. My last meeting with Eileen was in London, just a few years ago. We had tea together at her hotel, reminisced about Paris and Rome, where I used to see her and Jerry most years but with some gaps. There were three three-month spells in New York in the Sixties; there were other occasions later on when Eileen asked me over but regrettably I was not free to go.

PG:
So which photographers were you working with?

JK:
Probably the best known was Richard Avedon. The first time that I worked with him was for a shoot with *Harper's Bazaar*,[1] a wonderful magazine, with the best photographic pages at that time – the mid-Sixties. I remember he had asked to see me beforehand. I took a few photographs, but he said he didn't need to see them. We chatted and he peered over his spectacles, wired with enthusiasm. On the appointed day of the shoot, as I walked into Avedon's studio, reverberating with the sounds of jazz, it struck me that this felt like walking onto a Hollywood set. Jean Shrimpton was already there, in a sumptuous

---

1 'The Wilder Shores of Chic', August 1964

evening dress of floating chiffon, looking beautiful. She was the lead model for the shoot. The studio seemed to have the biggest team of assistants, under Dick's direction, moving big lights, operating wind machines, and touching up the all-white backdrop. There was also a team from the magazine – the fashion editor with several assistants, then many minions running around trying to follow orders. The whole atmosphere was that of a very, very important production, with a very important person. Unfortunately, my outfits were daywear and not particularly glamorous; however, they were expensive and stylish, with boots. I had to practise what we were going to do, which was to run in front of the backdrop and leap over a chosen spot, at the same time looking in the right direction and allowing the wind machine to do its thing, blowing hair and a chiffon scarf in just the right place! It took forever to achieve just a few photographs. The make-up artist and the hairdresser were terrific and knew all about shoots and the big difference between reality and the fantasy under big lights. Dick was gorgeous to work with – electric, lit up, and so alive. And he knew exactly what he was doing and how to get what he wanted. He was fearless with fashion editors who dared to have their own ideas of what we should do. There could be heated arguments, with the editor getting quite red in the face. Of course Dick did exactly what he wanted. Over the years that followed, Avedon asked me to work with him on several occasions. I remember Eileen Ford calling me when I was staying in Beverly Hills on my way to Polynesia. I couldn't free myself and had to turn him down. Anyway, to work with the great man was a privilege.

PG:
Thinking of American photographers, tell me about working with some of the other exceptional talents in New York, such as Bob Richardson and Saul Leiter.

JK:
Bob Richardson was significant for me. This was during my second New York stretch. Eileen Ford told me that this photographer was extremely keen on me, having seen me in various publications from England and from Europe, and would I go to his studio to see him. I went to the address she gave me, a warehouse building, and took the lift up to a black double door that stated 'Richardson Studio'. The door had barely opened a crack when Bob said, 'Aaahhh, Jill, come in.'

Bob was tall and thin, quite pale. He was dressed in black denims and an old sweater, and looked sort of gangly. Then his face broke into a huge smile and he said, 'I have been dying to meet you. Come in.' He then told me he did not need to see pictures, made us a cup of coffee, and introduced me to Norma, his wife. Bob had a gentle purring voice, whereas Norma's was strong, reflecting her personality, respectful but in charge. Bob did a lot of staring and smiling, secretly. I could tell that, yes, I would be working with him.

The first job that I did with him was in the studio and a favourite model of his called Donna Mitchell was there. She reminded me of a silent movie star, with a tragic quality. She had a very particular air of mystery, suggesting an inner depth that Bob responded to. I worked on a few jobs with Bob before an important big spread came up for American *Harper's Bazaar*, which was for sure my favourite American magazine. It had strong fashion spreads, two great art directors - Ruth Ansel and Bea Feitler - and a couple of very cool fashion editors, one of whom was willing to work with Bob despite his reputation as a difficult personality, which I witnessed in action and understood. When we worked together, I experienced a strong connection - a sort of magic started to happen, creating a mood, developing this intense atmosphere. But if a fashion editor popped in to fuss, or straighten a garment, it could totally break the spell. Bob would get very upset, angry, at this lack of instinct. He is reputed to have once locked a fashion editor in a cupboard, to keep her out of the way!

The next shoot would be on Long Island.[2] There were many meetings and trying-on of clothes at the *Bazaar* offices. We were to stay in a lovely country hotel, a young actor would be coming as well as Bob's favourite fashion editor and, very importantly, Norma, who had a great sense of style, knew Bob's every vibe, and also was incredible with make-up. Of course, these were still the days when freelance make-up artists were rarely used on a shoot - hairdressers yes, but make-up artists no. So Norma was key to creating a particular and unique look. The shoot had a strong character, a strong look. Black eyes suited me, but Norma did something different, suggesting that the eyeline went down rather than up. We practised until we had it right. I looked ethereal rather than tragic - and the clothes were secondary to what became a lovely story. Bob was in love with me, though this was only expressed obliquely, in looks and a tender voice. He would chuckle in his throat and give that purr as the photograph was being created; then a touch and a thank-you when we had it in the can. With Paul, the beautiful, quiet young actor-model I was working with, we achieved maybe two scenarios in a day. Time and mood were so important, and we had both. The light was gentle, sometimes grey. Bob managed in the resulting pictures to evoke a strong atmosphere

2 'Beached: A Seaside Scenario', August 1964

and an intense sense of the relationship between Paul and myself. As if we were in a film, the accompanying editorial cast us as Anna and Roberto, and even gave us a few enigmatic fragments of dialogue. Thinking back on that moment, it seemed like we had stepped into a dream.

PG:
Jill, I am fascinated to hear you evoke the great intensity of your work.

JK:
It was so strange, this freelance world that I lived in, always being so aware of giving everything to that instant – the click of the camera – that freezes the moment and seizes it forever. The days of a shoot all come down to capturing the essence of the moods and emotions that are built up between photographer and model. Bob was one of my favourites and we had a special rapport. He somehow made you bare your soul and invest your very being in the picture. It was joyous to work with him. I was early one day, in time to see Bob with his gangly lope coming down the street. He was hotly followed by Terry, his young son, whose curly hair bounced as he ran, holding on to Lucky – the giant poodle – with the same crazy, curly coat. Norma followed them, seemingly deep in thought. These were good days. I worked with Bob in New York, then in London for British *Vogue*. He took one of my favourite pictures – me in a peach-coloured Afghan coat, carrying a transistor radio – a wonderful touch, which gave me permission to act as if I was lost in the music.[3] Another *Vogue* spread that we did was set in a house in London. The look was a party scene, exotic, hinting at a decadent orgy. A beautiful male model was lying on the floor with Donna Mitchell, Sue Murray, and myself draped on top of him. The funny thing is that Beatrix Miller, then editor of British *Vogue*, had rung me up the evening before and said, 'Jill, can you help me please. Don't let Bob make the pictures look druggy.' The fact is that they did look druggy; Beatrix Miller's prediction proved justified and the pictures were 'killed', as they say in the magazine world. Fortunately, a few frames from the shoot were published in 2004 in Robin Muir's book, *Unseen Vogue*. We also worked in Brighton at the Royal Pavilion, journeying down from London by train. These pictures were all about lounging on chaises-longues.[4] I didn't know, until a later Paris shoot for French *Vogue*, how vulnerable Bob was. I was living in Paris by then. Norma called me to say that Bob wasn't well. He was going through a psychotic episode, so the shoot was postponed. We completed it eventually, a series of night shots against

---

3 September 15th 1966
4 The shoot was on May 2nd 1967. The pictures were not published.

the huge statues by Maillol that had recently been installed around the Tuileries Garden. There were some beautiful images – vivid-coloured evening dresses set against the dark statues, with white doves silhouetted against the night sky.[5] However, cracks were appearing and the pressure Bob put himself under was harsh. I wanted to just give him a hug.

PG:
And what about Saul Leiter?

JK:
Actually, I first met him in England. Saul Leiter was a strange and deep man, not at all like any other photographer I had worked with. When I first met him, he was lying down, on his stomach, in a field of wild flowers. The job was an advertising session for Mary Quant's Ginger Group, art directed by Tom Wolsey, who I knew. We were introduced and Saul lumbered clumsily to his feet, a bulky frame, totally dishevelled and a bit greasy. We said hello, and discussed what Tom wanted for this ad. I looked at the outfit and put on make-up to suit – pale face and brown eyelids, no false eyelashes – in the van that we came in, which was full of stuff, and rails, and mirrors. I discovered that Tom was quietly stressed. He told me that Saul had lain in this field for three days, trying to get inspiration: 'This is costing money!' Tom retorted. There was a car as a prop and I seem to remember trying, to no avail, various situations – leaning, sitting with door open, and so on – when, almost in desperation, I sat down and leant against the front wheel. Well, Saul sprang to life, taking pictures – click, click, click – until he had it, and I knew he had. He worked with a small, hand-held camera. I don't think I ever saw a tripod.

I always go beneath the skin of people and Saul was a gentle man and talented. The next time I worked with him was for a beauty picture for British *Vogue*. We met up at the *Vogue* studios. The outfit was a white shirt, and a tight skirt was chosen, not expected to be in shot, but just in case. Simple make-up and pulled-back hair was the look. Saul did not want a studio portrait. We went down in the lift and out into Hanover Square. There were newly installed parking meters, much to everyone's fury. I leant against one and Saul requested a pair of glasses, which I put on, peering over them. Then click, click, click, the picture was done in five minutes. We also did a cover for British *Vogue*[6] with a new Dynel wig, very long silver hair, which did look

---

5 'Robes noctambules', September 1967
6 October 1st 1966

amazing. And we shot fashion for the *Weekend Telegraph* magazine with Cherry Twiss. Cherry came up with great location ideas and she put us together for a trip to the Highlands of Scotland.[7] It worked out really well. Saul responded with such sensitivity to the light and to the atmosphere of the settings. The clothes were made of fine wools and fine tweeds. We stayed up there for about five days, photographing in glens and hills and castles. What I remember most, though, was getting to know this man, Saul Leiter. We would talk in the evenings, talk philosophy, and I discovered that he was a very learned man. He had trained as a rabbi. Saul had an immense, unhurried charm.

PG:

You remind me how the best pictures will always express the spirit of the photographer. It must have been so interesting to experience such different approaches.

JK:

It was indeed. Another American I worked with, a very different personality, was Bert Stern. He was a dynamic, high-profile, highly successful commercial photographer at this time, running a big studio for advertising, fashion, portrait, and other editorial work. I did several jobs with him. The first was editorial and I remember thinking, 'Wow'. I knew he had made those remarkable pictures of Marilyn Monroe for *Vogue* shortly before she died; but he wasn't what I expected, though I didn't really know what to expect. He was quite swarthy, very male, with dark hair and good eyes. He was studying me all the time, quietly scrutinising me, and while we worked together I felt slightly unsure. Maybe that was a good thing.

The last job was a very expensive advertisement and I had to wear a beautiful silk slip and gown, very Hollywood. There were lots of hair and make-up people, so I was primped and pampered. Then I was shown the agency art director's drawing, which was to be followed precisely. It showed me lying on a big bed, on my back, hair spilling over the end of the bed with my legs up, away from the camera, ankles crossed. So, into position, with lots of tweaks from the stylists: more powder; move the hair; place props, which must not show, under my calves so that I could stay in position. Then there was a problem. Bert could see my body stocking. So that had to come off. Then, when I settled in position again, there was another problem. My nipples showed. There followed a hilarious palaver of taping nipples with flesh-coloured tape. This wouldn't be an issue today as shoots

7   'The fashionable weekend', August 19th 1966

A LUXURY—but a very useful one—is a long coat to put over the long skirts of the country against its dewy evening chill. At Aberuchill Castle (see also photograph on page 16), guest wears one in bottle-green wool, buttoned down the front, 47gns, by Maggi Shepherd, 31 Maddox Street, London, W1 (not shown, matching long skirt and jerkin top to wear under it, $32\frac{1}{2}$gns). At the neck here: green silk scarf with white pin dots, £3 5s at Liberty's, Regent Street, London, W1

'The fashionable weekend', by Saul Leiter, *Weekend Telegraph*, August 19th 1966

are much more laid back about such things, but eventually all was deemed polite enough for the client. The shoot, when we eventually started, didn't take long, unlike the careful preparations beforehand. I had to look at Bert from this head-back position while he shot from a low stepladder. I did get to see the photograph, though I don't have a tear sheet of it now, and it was terrific, both classy and seductive.

PG:
Jill, you must tell me also about working with William Klein.

JK:
The first time I noticed William Klein, his crazy, wonderful photographs taken in the streets of Tokyo were displayed in the windows of Liberty in Regent Street – huge black and white, gritty, often blurred images portraying the bustle of life on the move. Before long, I worked with him in Paris. I had done a movie casting in Saint-Germain for a role in his film, *Qui êtes-vous, Polly Maggoo?*, which I didn't get. He said, generously, that I looked too intelligent! The film, released in 1966, was a satirical art-house project spoofing the fashion world. Klein always had an ambivalence about fashion and injected that subversive spirit into his shoots. Then, the *Weekend Telegraph* magazine booked me for the feature entitled 'Is Paris dead?'[8] This was a tongue-in-cheek story with Cherry Twiss about the possible demise of Paris haute couture. London was abuzz with music, theatre, and street style, and seemed to be the centre of everything. The young trendsetters weren't interested in what was happening on the other side of the Channel. The lead image was of a line of models in classic couture clothes, walking beside a horse-drawn hearse with the Eiffel Tower in the background. This made a striking spread, together with the bold, challenging title, though the clear response made by the feature was a powerful 'Non!' Paris couture was very much holding its own. The next day, in Bill's studio, I had to confront a coffin. I remember the make-up was good and the outfit was a stunning bright pink cape with hood, designed by Pierre Cardin. Bill asked me to step into the coffin and lie down; then the fashion team surrounded me with red roses. It was spooky. I had to relax, which was easy, lying down in the coffin, letting the team fiddle and arrange the flowers until Bill was satisfied. I reminded myself that I was not dead yet! It was hard not to get the giggles as Bill was very funny. This photograph was used on the cover, framed in black, with the title in Gothic type. It was quite stunning and definitely different. Amazingly, thirty years

8   September 3rd 1965

later, to celebrate the anniversary of the *Telegraph* magazine, it was used again, this time against a white background.[9] I worked in Paris with Bill on other occasions; the last time I saw him, for a walk and a chat, was just after the memorial for Helmut Newton in the Palais Royal theatre in 2004. This context gave a particular poignancy to my recollections of working with Bill all those years before on the 'Is Paris dead?' shoot.

9 September 3rd 1994

The Collections: is Paris dead?

'The Collections: is Paris dead?', by William Klein,
Weekend Telegraph, September 3rd 1965

'the sheen age', by Helmut Newton for Goya advertising campaign, *Nova*, April 1967

Helmut Newton

from Waterloo Station to Saint-Tropez and Tunisia –
a heatwave in the studio – a futuristic laboratory –
Helmut's electric energy

PG:

Jill, you mention Helmut Newton. You did some great work with him in the Sixties, when he was already well respected in the business but before he achieved the huge profile he enjoyed from the mid-Seventies onwards. Tell me about those pictures, and what it was like working with him.

JK:

Helmut goes down in history as one of the major fashion photographers of all time. There was no one like him and I personally thought he was great. I remember my ignorance when I was first asked to work with him on a shoot for *Queen*.[1] I said, 'Who is Helmut Newton? Can I see some of his work?' He had been working for Australian *Vogue* and a copy was sent over. The fashion feature that I saw was shot on location and made a good impression on me. This guy can take pictures, I thought, so I said yes. He was by then based in Paris, but worked occasionally in England, and now for *Queen*, for the first time.

He wanted to do a shoot at Waterloo Station, on deserted platforms. In those days there were still steam trains and one picture made a feature of the clouds of steam. I was to look very Forties - elegant and with waved hair. It was arranged for me to go to Leonard's salon in Brook Street to have my hair washed and set. I had to be there at 6.00am. My hair was set in tiny rollers, then combed out to create waves. This made it look much shorter, and it certainly did achieve a nostalgic Hollywood film star look. There was a second model for this job, with dark hair in contrast to mine. The shoot was great, with lots of good humour, but Helmut knew exactly what he wanted; and it was quite clear that a rapport developed. I was standing on the platform; then sitting on a luggage trolley; then on the train, with the images shot through the window. It resulted in a great feature with plenty of atmosphere. I remember it vividly after all these years, though I haven't seen those pictures again. That was the beginning of my working relationship with Helmut.

---

1 'Travellin' on', January 13th 1965

I was always excited when a message came through for a job with Helmut. There was a big ad campaign for Chemstrand, the fabric manufacturer, set up by, I think, Collett Dickenson Pearce, a very creative advertising agency with cool art directors. The campaign ran over a few years and involved a series of memorable pictures. It was cast with five girls. We were all blonde. The location was to be the South of France, and we went first to Saint-Tropez and then to the long empty sands of Pampelonne Beach, eating at the small, rustic Club 55 at the beginning of the charming Patrice's culinary career.

Helmut created an incredibly sensual mood in those pictures. They were sexy, yet in a subtle, sophisticated way. I recall one picture where we were all in wet suits, with masks. For another we all wore dark glasses, while in yet another our skin glistened with oil. They were groundbreaking and always wonderful. Helmut had us fold our bodies together like sexy seals, basking in the sun. We also went to Hammamet in Tunisia, where he took photographs in the village, and on a later trip to Djerba, which then had only a couple of hotels. There we posed on this giant sand bar. I stayed behind with one of the models to do a few swimsuit shots for *Vogue* – no accessories, just light and sand, and natural hair.[2] Helmut was a master of his craft, and the pictures were very good – straightforward yet impactful.

One day to remember was the corridor shoot for *Queen*.[3] I was asked to be at Bowater House in Knightsbridge. I was shown down to the bowels of the building where Helmut was setting up in a modern corridor, with tripod and assistant. I looked at the clothes – simple, young suits. We decided that hair should be long, straight, and natural. So how were we going to make this interesting? I was never satisfied with just standing as a fashion plate; nor was Helmut. Something had to happen. Well, the first extra ingredient was a wind machine, which immediately animated the look. Helmut said he wanted me in mid-stride, as if I was walking down the corridor. I wanted to use the door handle to give a sense of being off balance, so we secured the handle on the other side which meant that I could pull on it, giving the appearance of being about to stride through the door. This was great and we were on a roll. The resulting pictures proved to be quite different from anything done before. I remember being at *Vogue* after they came out and Bailey said, 'Great spread, Jill', looking, I thought, as though what he really wanted to ask was, 'How did you come up with that?'

---

2 'Sea change – bare new elements', April 1st 1966
3 'Player's please', January 6th 1966

'When the stripes come marching in - five times jazzier!', by Helmut Newton
for Chemstrand advertising campaign, *Sunday Times Colour Magazine*, April 11th 1966

PG:
Jill, do describe Helmut and what made him special.

JK:
Helmut was a live wire. He was vibrant and very charming. With a slight build, dark brown hair with a natural 'cowlick', and thick-framed glasses, Helmut dressed French casual in simple open-neck shirts and chinos, sweater to hand or a Parka in winter. He had an air of *passe-partout*, expensive, understated; most of all, he wore a smile. He was insatiably curious and would peer at me with a quizzical look. You really wanted to do your best for him. His funny two-tone laugh was sweet excitement and he was the most enthusiastic photographer. An almost electric energy emanated from him. He also showed a generosity of spirit quite rare in photographers, building a real sense of involvement with the team. He would make sure that the magazine or client allowed for him to stay in lovely hotels or villas and to eat good food in the kind of restaurants - authentic and unpretentious - that he appreciated; and he would invite us to eat together. He was not a bit ostentatious, always one hundred per cent committed. He was a lovely friend and many a trip benefited from the company of June, his bright and characterful wife.

In the spring of 1965, we had a story to achieve for British *Vogue*. We had done quite a number of spreads for *Queen* and *Elle*, as well as glossy advertising spreads for which Helmut had carte blanche to go anywhere he chose. For this story for *Vogue* he had been given free rein, and when I arrived at the *Vogue* studios, there was a room-set in place. It was a bright, all-white bedroom, with a tropical feel suggested by a ceiling fan - of the type you associate with colonial residences. Beside the big bed with its white cover was a small table with a fan and a simple stool. For the various shots, Helmut used a number of different props - a bottle of Coca Cola and glass, a hotel key, a small radio, a packet of cigarettes and a lighter, all typical playful Helmut touches. For some of the shots, he pinned photographs of me onto the wall above the bed. He also included notes, written in his looping handwriting, that added to the underlying storyline

We had our hugs; then we looked at the clothes. But the important part was the mood and vibe for these pictures. In the first outfit, I settled back on the bed, in my imaginary room, with Helmut opposite me. His Nikon was on the tripod and we started. The mood was easy. Helmut said, 'Imagine that it's incredibly hot, darling.' His curious sort of American, Australian, hint-of-German accented voice was encouraging me to give, give, give. I know in my being when a picture is happening, when we have got it, and when to keep going. The

Sunsoaked and indolent, all I can bear to wear in the evening is my crepe jumpsuit. All-in-one, with a halter neck, no back. Summerflower colours on white; about 12½ gns., Foale & Tuffin, 1 Marlborough Ct. Shoes, Giusti, 7 gns., Fortnum & Mason

'Heatwave Holiday', by Helmut Newton, British *Vogue* July 1965

strange but very powerful thing about Helmut was that energy just vibrated out of him. He got very excited, totally engrossed in making his picture; the build-up reached a peak, and then the moment was captured, at just the right time. He would sit with his knees out to either side of the tripod, on a stool; then he would stand up, push his lock of dark hair to the side and give me a kiss – 'Thank you, darling, that was beautiful.' So, you see, I always pulled the stops out for him. One of the pictures from the shoot is a great favourite of mine. I had on a sort of all-in-one crepe halter-neck jumpsuit. The brief was the same, that it was hot as hell. I thought of insane heat, forgot about the outfit, and just flopped, sprawled out on my front across the bed, naturally spreading my arms. Helmut shot from high above, with the silhouette of the ceiling fan adding a graphic element to the composition. He tweaked my position, face to this side, eyes closed, hair mussed; then we were away. I felt completely involved in the role and the resulting photograph was much more than a conventional fashion picture. In the published feature, it faced a picture of me in a tiny nightdress, my skin oiled, but this time the pose was reversed with me lying, stretched out on my back. The pictures were really inventive and atmospheric – that dramatic angle, me lying down, limbs akimbo, sexy, hot, and asleep. The feature 'Heatwave Holiday'[4] filled ten pages.

PG:
You clearly made a dynamic team.

JK:
I think I could say that Helmut was the most powerful photographer that I worked with. He so knew what he was doing. His sensitivity to atmosphere was exceptional; and he had a remarkable psychological grasp, both of the now and of the future, by which I mean he seemed always one step ahead of what was happening. I remember a shoot in the mews behind the American Embassy in London's Grosvenor Square. The frame was filled – me, with sunglasses, surrounded by a street packed with paparazzi. This was way ahead – recreating the buzz of photographers in the Via Veneto, capturing images of Rome nightlife as immortalised by Fellini in *La Dolce Vita*. I considered myself lucky to be a top favourite of his.

Helmut's wonderful imagination was impressive, along with his meticulous attention to detail and his great enthusiasm. We did a spectacular futuristic shoot in London for an advertisement for

---

4 July 1965

Goya lipstick, 'The Sheen Age', published in the spring of 1967.[5] It took place in Cornel Lucas's studio, which was a big space. I turned up and walked in to find not a background paper and stool but a shining, elaborate, highly stylised science laboratory set. Lots of spiralling glass tubes, clamps, mixing jars, and burners were all set against a clean, space-age background. Wow! It looked so cool. The assistant was being directed by Helmut, who looked through his camera, fixed on its tripod: 'Move that one half an inch to the left', and so on. After a big kiss hello, the stylist showed me a few outfits, all silver, which I tried on and then, after some deliberation, made the decision as to which looked and felt the best – an all-in-one jumpsuit. I went up to the gallery, which had dressing tables and mirrors surrounded by light bulbs. The music was turned on. There was a make-up artist on this job, as it was a beauty shot, but we did it together, so that I preserved my particular look: hair down and back-combed to give a lift, big, dark eyes, and pale, lustrous lips. Once it was done, I went down to show Helmut. Great, okay, ready to go. I eased myself into the silver second-skin outfit. I was very pleased with the way it looked. It felt modern and had real impact. I slipped into my lab, behind shelves of glass, and felt like the strong woman scientist. Helmut loved strong women; he never went for pretty, always for power. This look was unique to him. I think that is one of the reasons why his work is so recognisable. He did produce remarkable and unforgettable images. There are many pictures I made with him that I remember with pride. Helmut was the first fashion photographer to shine skin with oil, and he loved girls in dark glasses. His images made a forceful statement. The message was an impactful one: 'Here I am; I'm a beautiful, powerful, capable woman.' I loved the man.

---

5 British *Vogue*, April 1st 1967; *Nova*, April 1967

THINGS HAVE TOUGHENED UP IN THE HOT-HOUSE OF FASHION

All the best swimsuits are red, white and blue this year. Hence the patriotic atmosphere supplied by the Guards.   Swimsuit by Marks & Spencer, 39s. 11d.

The hectic world of a photogenic blonde..

'The hectic world of a photogenic blonde', by John Cowan,
Daily Mirror, May 29th 1963

Full circle

riding with the Life Guards – naked on a white horse –
racing an E-Type Jaguar – on horseback for Vogue

PG:
Jill, you were brought up with horses. Some of your most memorable pictures
feature horses. Life turned full circle. Tell me about these.

JK:
I love horses. I was at ease with horses; I had an appreciation of their
beauty and of their amazing instinct and intuition. Anyone who has
ever had a horse, and I don't mean just going to a riding school but
who has really looked after them and respected them, will tell you,
as I do, that the connection is extraordinary. For me, the best part of
it all was the exhilarating sense of freedom that I experienced when
riding cross- country, jumping hedges and ditches and dykes. Of
course, I fell off a lot, taking the tumbles, but I just love riding in the
landscape, whatever the weather.

So, yes, there were many horse shoots. John cooked up the idea of
me riding bareback in a swimsuit along London's Constitution Hill,
with a troop of Life Guards in the background. We had to plan this
carefully, as we would certainly be stopped. So I was in this swimsuit,
with vertical red, white and blue stripes, astride a gorgeous white
horse, waiting discreetly with a coat over my shoulders. John was at
the ready, all set to shoot pictures from the moving Land Rover, with
his assistant at the wheel. When I saw John coming into position
just in front of the Life Guards, I cast the coat aside, and positioned
myself between vehicle and horses, actually trotting at quite a pace.
Of course, very soon we were instructed to get out of the way. Barely
a roll of film and definitely no take two. This was for a feature for the
Daily Mirror with the title 'The hectic world of a photogenic blonde'.[1]
It was the picture that sowed the seed to try and do something really
beautiful with me and a horse.

The perfect opportunity came later the following year, in 1964, when
we prepared to do a shoot for *Queen* with me naked, bareback on a
horse at the water's edge. I was very worried about taking my clothes
off but willing to trust John. The art director was Tom Wolsey, and

_____

1 May 29th 1963

he was excited about taking a set of pictures without any fashion element or other restriction, just as a creative exercise. We set off for Sandwich Bay in Kent. There was a local stable with which we had arranged the loan of a pretty dappled grey, almost white, with a long mane. They met us on the sands. John, the stable girl, John's assistant, and I were in fact the only people around. This allowed me to relax, and once again I stripped off – this time completely naked, with a coat round me until we were ready. I tried to forget about myself and just be at one with the horse. I lost my self-consciousness in the delight of feeling so close to this wonderful creature – it was just me, the horse, and the elements. The shoot came together and we knew we had captured something very authentic and very special. For once, I didn't have to keep changing; there was a great sense of freedom, and the pictures just evolved. It was agreed that I could inspect the pictures before they went off. When I saw the results back in London, they were really beautiful – sensual and natural. So I was nervous, but happy about them. They ran over two spreads the following May with the title 'An olde English love affair'[2] and were also taken up by the magazine *Adam* in France and by *Twen*, a great German magazine that featured terrific photography.

PG:
You are clearly fearless on horseback. You must have been the best candidate for such shots.

JK:
I guess so. Another memorable time on horseback was a shoot with Norman Parkinson. I was very fond of Parks. We were doing a National Benzole ad for Super National petrol. The campaign was a big project, with magazine placements, television ads, and huge billboard images around London. The location was Camber Sands in Kent. I would be galloping along in the surf at the water's edge, while a young man would be racing me in a white, open-top E-Type Jaguar on the sands. Parks was in another car, so that he could take pictures on the move. At one point, we stopped for half an hour to have tea in the café. 'Darling Jillykins,' said Parks – he often called me Jillykins – 'I think we've got it, but we'll do a few more.' However, a shock awaited us. When we got back to the Jaguar, which had been left in situ, it wouldn't move. Oh my God! The tide had turned and the sand had started to turn soggy. The more we tried to rev the Jag out of this situation, with everyone pushing from behind, the more it sank in, now immersed up to its hub caps. We tried using a Land Rover and tow ropes but, as the tide

---

2 May 19th 1965

AN OLDE ENGLISH LOVE AFFAIR

Man and horse has always been a matter of expediency. True Richard III offered his kingdom for one, which is as far as a man could go in deference to a horse but quite misleading as to the real relationship in view of his dire circumstances at the time. Who could doubt that he would have opted for a Mini had it been possible, which would have spoiled Shakespeare's line but would have increased Richard's chances of an accelerated exit. But with English women the horse has indisputably been an affair of the heart, a great love affair that blossoms in the pony club and continues with the hunt. What perfect relationships can be seen at a point-to-point whereas with a man it's so obvious they're just good friends.

To a woman a horse is also a confidant and, as John Cowan's photographs on these pages show, there are no secrets beween them. It's also interesting to note that despite current trends, nudes can be beautiful.

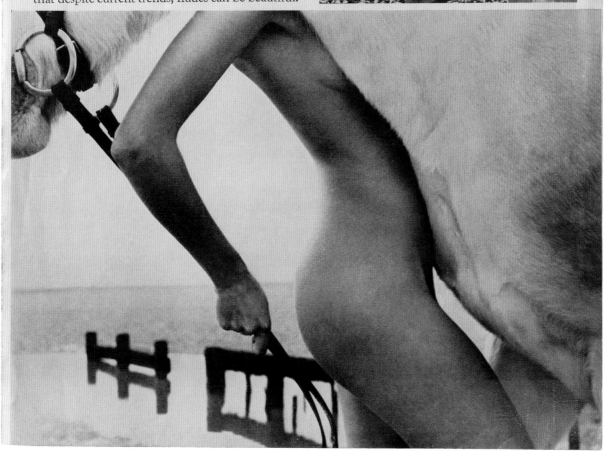

'An olde English love affair', by John Cowan, *Queen*, May 19th 1965
Overleaf: Jill, by Norman Parkinson for Super National advertising campaign, September 23rd 1963

came in around our ankles, we faced the ghastly realisation that the sea was going to claim this beautiful car. We had to call off attempts to pull it free; the man from Jaguar was extremely upset; the car was ruined; but Parks had his picture.

PG:
And there was that great Vernier shoot for Vogue. *What can you tell me about that?*

JK:
The most gorgeous and atmospheric photograph with a horse was taken by Eugene Vernier, for British *Vogue*.[3] Gene, as I used to call him, was French, with a small moustache and vibrant, dark, twinkly eyes. He was a very good photographer, but, importantly, he was also a sweet and lovely man, both charming and clever, a joy to work with.

We met up in the King's Road, Chelsea. I parked my purple Mini at World's End and bumped into Gene on the way to his fabulous studio nearby. It was big enough to drive cars into. I believe he did quite a lot of advertising work. I also worked there with Helmut on more than one occasion, once, memorably, submerged in a fish tank.

The planned shoot was a peach. I had been told that the photograph would be with or on a horse. I guess I was a natural choice as I so love horses. We drove off to the location in the van, which was full of the usual clobber – the clothes, the cameras, the mirror, the white reflector, a stepladder, and umbrellas. We were a nice, small team: Gene, his assistant, the fashion editor, a really good-looking male model, and myself. We met up with a woman Gene knew, with two horses from her stables, each about 17 hands.

The location was gorgeous as it was a totally natural, unmanicured landscape. It was late summer and the grass was high. I really loved the idea for this picture. It was intended to conjure up thoughts of love and romance in the sun, maybe a picnic. Lovely Marit Allen was the fashion editor and she had wonderful instinct and taste. This was to be a single shot within a series on the theme of picnics with images by several photographers and she allowed me to have mussed hair and bare feet, giving more importance to the mood than to the clothes. The plan was to create something languid and natural. Having set the job up, Marit always stood back to let me and the photographer work together.

_____

3 'Picnics', July 1965

No pressure today. What we needed was a fabulous photograph, not to rush through six outfits. We had the gift of time. The male model and I rode around to get used to the horses; then I sat in the grass doing my make-up, trying to make it look as if I wasn't wearing any. The situation called for a natural look. The horse nuzzled my neck. Gene used to ride and so he too was at ease with horses, which ensured the atmosphere was relaxed. He chose a spot and we rode over to it. I remember imagining that I was here on a romantic, unhurried afternoon, that we had made love in the long grass; and I think the photograph captured this possibility. It was Gene's idea for the man to take his shirt off, mine to rough up my hair. Marit approved and allowed us to follow our instincts. I loved the end result. It was natural but strong, and I felt truly myself in this picture, while as a fashion photograph it told the necessary story for the shirt and culottes that were being featured. *Vogue* was very generous and gave it the double-page spread that I felt it deserved. Gene did a great job. Hugs all round!

Nous sommes au cœur des **MILLE ET UNE NUITS** ✳ ✳ en robes des **MILLE ET UNE FETES** C'est le pays d'Aladin, des jasmins blancs, des matins roses, des satins pourpres, des destins rouge et or. C'est un rêve. L'Orient. Et l'on y entre par la plus sublime des portes : Istanbul. Nous y voici : cette mer de coupoles devant la mer — la Marmara — c'est Istanbul vue des toits du Sérail où nous avons enlevé... une redingote de jeune sultane, en soie, d'un luxe « byzantin » (Détails page 156).

ELLENOEL

DE
NOS
ENVOYES
SPECIAUX
EN
TURQUIE
CLAUDE
BROUET
ET
J. COWAN

75

'Mille et une nuits - mille et une fêtes', by John Cowan, *Elle*, December 6th 1963

To Turkey for *Elle*

a great magazine team – on location in Istanbul and beyond –
John's appetite for risk

PG:
Jill, you have talked of great shots on location in England. But you also made stunning pictures in many foreign and sometimes far-flung locations.

JK:
The first truly exotic trip was to Turkey for *Elle* in October 1963.[1] John and I had by now won the confidence of *Elle* magazine's creative staff. They realised that we were a great team and could be trusted to produce a charismatic set of images on location. We had cut our teeth with several small location shoots in Paris; then we made a picture for them in the spirit of the 'Birds in Space' feature for the *Sunday Times*, but this time using a trapeze rather than a parachute. Peter Knapp, *Elle*'s terrific art director, and Hélène Lazareff, the editor-in-chief, called us in for a discussion about doing a big shoot in Turkey, with a good fashion editor, Claude Brouet, who we had already worked with. I was very excited about the trip – another country, full of history and with a rich culture so different from anything I knew. I always felt that opportunities to travel were a great privilege, a gift that I was so lucky to enjoy. Trips such as this were a great education.

It was decided that I would play the leading role in the pictures, but that French model Nicole de la Marge would join us. Conveniently for her, she was Peter Knapp's girlfriend. I had met her in the *Elle* studios. She was very easy-going and really knew her craft. The day came to fly to Istanbul. I remember thinking, when the aircraft doors opened – to a wall of heat and dust and unfamiliar, exotic, far-off sounds – that this trip would be amazing. We were met by a splendid uniformed gentleman with a full handlebar moustache. I gather he represented the tourist office and was appointed to act as our guide and guard. I nicknamed him the Tourist Man. He took us to a very modern hotel, and indeed stayed with us the whole time. We all took off on a location hunt for about four pictures in the city. We started shooting the next day, on some wonderful ancient steps. Clothes still had to be well shown and I had to do my own make-up and hair. As always, there was a small crowd of curious onlookers. Our second picture was to be

---

1 'Mille et une nuits – mille et une fêtes', December 6th 1963

at the city walls, with a mule and cart, and me on the cart. Halfway through this shoot, John asked the old driver if I could do a Ben Hur – that is to say he wanted me to stand on the cart holding the reins like a charioteer. John would be in another vehicle, driving alongside. I can't think why I felt no fear on these wild escapades; instead I felt great, found my balance well enough, and we ended up going at a hell of a lick, rattling along the cobbled street with me thinking, 'Only one long take here. I hope it's in the can.'

That evening our Tourist Man took us to eat local food – hummus, salads, roasted lamb, all absolutely delicious, a real education in tastes. Istanbul had streets that were heady with the smells of spices, fruit, herbs, and of course incredible coffee. We did some photographs the following day, at the oldest mosque in the city and in the biggest bath house. This was so beautiful, all lined with marble and with marble slabs to lie on while being scrubbed and massaged; the atmosphere was filled with steam and perfumed oils. There was a women's section and a separate men's section. At the end of the day, we all indulged in the experience.

Things were going well, but John wanted to do a photograph with a bear. The Tourist Man said, 'There are no bears.' This inevitably became a contest, with John determined to succeed in finding one. Of course there were bears, but the use of performing bears was by then illegal, for good reason, so they could only be found illicitly. The Tourist Man prevailed. We learned that the training was cruel but John was nonetheless furious and drank too much whisky. He put his glass down too forcefully and it broke, entering his wrist. I have never had such a shock – blood spurted from the wound. I leapt to it, being practical, and made a tourniquet for his arm with towels around his wrist and a bar of dry soap in his inner elbow, tied with a stocking, after which I called the desk for an ambulance, called his assistant, Allan Ballard, and also Claude Brouet, who rushed to the scene. John was getting weak. Luckily, the ambulance arrived fast and took him off to the American Hospital.

This was a very scary incident. We lost a day while he was strapped up and given painkillers, but then it was back to work pretty much as usual, though Allan would set up the tripod and camera and take the shots once John had looked through the viewfinder to check everything and then give the instruction. Nicole had now arrived and John had in mind a shot with her standing among fishermen in a smallish boat on the Bosphorus. She looked great. John was still weak, so Allan and I helped to get the picture done.

The next plan was to go up into the mountains, to a place called Göreme, the city of the sandstone churches. We had to fly to Kayseri, stay a night there, and then travel in a Land Rover to our destination. We couldn't stay long in case we got cut off by snow. It was incredible, a wild, biblical landscape. The ever-present Tourist Man had a gun in case of bandits. I did a photograph in the sandstone churches, amazingly chipped and carved out of the rock, the interiors covered with faded paintings and frescoes. These were early Christian churches. We visited one of the villages and had to drive down a dry riverbed to get there. Children came pouring out to greet us, so many of them, all looking the same. Apparently the village got cut off for months every winter by the bad weather, making this a very closed, inbred community. Our next mission was to photograph with the Turkish cavalry, and for this we returned to Istanbul. The last photograph was pretty incredible as an expression of sheer energy. The cavalry used heavy horses and John wanted Nicole and me to be at the front to either side, with the cavalry doing a charge between us. They thundered through, churning up the dust, close enough for us to feel hot breath. We simply trusted the truism that a horse will never tread on a human being if it can possibly avoid it.

VOGUE's EYE VIEW:
THE GIRL WHO WENT
OUT IN THE COLD

JOHN COWAN

In a big, glorious bundle of shaggy white lamb, a girl in the very limit of cold—a girl at the top of the world. Arctic world —a soundless, windless place like the inside of an enormous diamond, where nothing falls; nothing blows . . . where children play together, and make no noise . . . where all sense of time and distance is reshaped by days that are twenty-four hours of light, and the flat, unchanging horizon makes remote islands seem within quick reach . . . where the sky hangs as low as a bright-blue stage backdrop, sewn forever to an improbable sheet of white . . . where the refraction of sun on the blinking brilliance of snow and ice spangles the entire world in glacial pastel shadows. This glittering world—scene of the next fourteen pages. (Hooded Mongolian lamb parka by Revillon. Saks Fifth Avenue; Neiman Marcus. Hansen gloves.)

Above and pp. 102-103: 'The girl who went out in the cold', by John Cowan,
American *Vogue*, November 1st 1964

To the Arctic for American *Vogue*

a telegram from Diana Vreeland – preparations in New York –
the long journey via Toronto and Anchorage – Gerry the Mountie –
snow and ice floes as far as the eye can see, and a polar bear –
shooting fashion in sub-zero temperatures

PG:
Wonderful adventures. And what about your first job for Diana Vreeland,
newly arrived at American Vogue; *wasn't it Vreeland who sent you to the*
Arctic?

JK:
Yes. There had been a meeting with her on my trip to New York in the
spring of 1964, soon after John's 'The Interpretation of Impact through
Energy' exhibition. She had been quite taken by John, and ideas for
trips had been discussed, including shooting high fashion in the
Arctic landscape.[1] There had been a lot of communication. Then the
day arrived when John and I received a telegram from Diana Vreeland
to say the Arctic trip was confirmed. We were incredibly excited. The
Vogue team was bowled over by the challenge and realised it couldn't
be achieved without the help of the military. It was everything that
Vreeland loved – a fantastic, exotic idea that appealed to her appetite
for surprise and for the truly groundbreaking. Nobody had done a
fashion shoot in the Artic before; nor, as far as I am aware, has anyone
done it since.

John spent a lot of time with camera and film experts, anticipating
the challenges of photographing at below-zero temperatures. I struck
out a month in my diary. We flew to New York and were booked in
to the St Regis hotel in Manhattan, which was very smart and very
comfortable. The vision that sticks in my mind is of Salvador Dalí,
sitting in a huge high-backed chair by the elevators and thus able to
chat to people coming and going. We were there for a week and Dalí
seemed to be positioned by that elevator much of the time.

Vogue was really well organised and the fashion team had found
appropriate clothes, following the brief that everything should be

---

1 'The girl who went out in the cold', November 1st 1964

pale – cream, white, silver, and grey. There were feathers and sequins, leotards and furs, boots and gloves. I had to try things on and a choice was eventually made. Each outfit was bagged up with appropriate boots and accessories. I suppose there must have been a couple of dozen outfits. Another girl was also booked. Our party – John, his assistant Allan, the gutsy editor-at-large Mary Kruming, the back-up model Antonia Boeckesteyn, and me – was sent over to a military outfitters. They helped us with polar-condition Parkas and boots, mittens and hats. We were given wonderful silk thermal vests with long sleeves and 'long johns'. The great thing about these items was their lightness and the fact that they were very thin, so as not to look bulky under the outfits; and apparently they would be life-savingly warm.

We were nearly set to go and the last discussion in Vreeland's office was make-up. This was hugely important, as the wrong make-up with these clothes would completely alter the mood. I did a make-up to show an idea. Vreeland's strong, imperious gaze, with her glittering black eyes, took me in – pale face, strong eyes, white under the brows, no lipstick. It was decided definitely no red lips; the eyes should be even more dramatic; I should take liquid eyeliner for more definition, to bring the lines a little further out; I should add silver with some outfits, on lids and under the brow; I should use pale lipstick that would be in keeping with the drama of an Ice Queen, a superior being. A blusher should subtly shade the cheeks, but not a hint of pink. An assistant was duly sent out to buy make-up, not forgetting a base and translucent powder.

PG:
I guess you had to be particularly well prepared for a trip such as this.

JK:
Yes, this was exceptional, but we were now finally set to go. Feeling the butterflies in our stomachs, the five of us took off on a scheduled flight from New York to Toronto, where we spent the night in order to be ready to fly out early in the morning on the next leg of our journey. As we approached the huge glass walls of the airport exit, we were met by an extraordinary sight. It was dark outside but from the inside I could see that the entire area of glass was covered with swarms of insects, attracted by the bright light. They were as big as horse flies, probably greenheads. We were met by cars and checked in to the modern hotel.

Our flight from Toronto the next morning was in a much smaller plane. We were heading north towards Anchorage and it was fascinating to look out over the changing landscape. We flew over forests, which became ever smaller, until we edged over the tundra and finally reached Alaska's largest city. Here, people disembarked and cargo was dropped off. Our group transferred to a large troop helicopter. Now we really started to feel as if we were closing in on our destination. This was my first time in a helicopter and the throb of the motor made my heart beat faster. We were flying much closer to the ground now and visibility was perfect. We were all transfixed by the landscape below. Now we were flying over water; the pilot asked us to look left and we saw two blue whales making their journey north. They resembled two torpedoes side by side just beneath the surface and they did indeed look blue as they swam through the sea. I felt very privileged and very humbled. All around was sea, now dotted with ice, which gradually became more and more dominant. Then we arrived at Frobisher Bay. A doctor disembarked and more supplies were dropped off. Next we transferred to a small plane and set off for our final destination, with a brief stop at Hall Beach radar station, where we took the opportunity to pull some extra layers of clothing from our cases as it was getting noticeably colder. We were soon airborne once again and flying north, towards the Arctic Circle. There was a red splash on the ice, an Inuit on a seal hunt. He seemed to be miles from anywhere, on the now-frozen sea, a small dot in pursuit of survival.

It was amazing. We were surrounded by ice and snow, the whole vast landscape uniformly white. A whoop of joy greeted the sight of one lone polar bear, trundling along, looking like a pat of butter on the white surface below. On to Resolute Bay on Cornwallis Island and a meteorological station on an American base inside the magnetic North Pole. It was light when we arrived – in fact we experienced the whole ten-day trip in the light, for this was the season of the midnight sun. I have no recollection of how long our journey took but eventually we saw a speck in the distance. As we got closer, we could recognise buildings – lots of Nissen huts and some much bigger settlements – as well as masts and electrical structures. My heart was pounding as we came in to land. Outside, I saw a couple of flags and a small group of people waiting for us. The engines were turned off. We had at last arrived, tired with exhilaration. John had a lot to prove, this being his first trip for American *Vogue*.

PG:
So you had finally arrived. What awaited you?

JK:
I looked around with awe. There was the wonderful sight of a Mountie standing to attention: hat, boots, shiny buttons on his jacket, and a

bright red stripe down the sides of his breeches. The jovial pilot and co-pilot helped us down the steps and I set foot on Arctic ice. I took a deep breath of burning cold air. Our party was introduced to Gerry, the Mountie, who would be at our disposal to help with everything. We sensed immediately that he was someone in whom we could trust absolutely and he turned out to be a wonderful character. Do you know, his beat, his area of responsibility, extended for thousands of square miles. The base was deliberately set up a long way from anywhere. There were about one hundred personnel working there, a tight community of scientists, communications specialists, meteorologists, engineers, electricians, plumbers, male nurses, cooks, a fitness coach, and so on. It was a male community and the work contracts lasted six months, no more, because of the risks of mental breakdowns in this extreme and isolated environment. The strange atmosphere was further exaggerated by the light patterns, with six months of darkness alternating with six months of light – a strange environment indeed. We were taken to our living accommodation, together with our personal luggage, by snowmobile – a thrilling ride. The clothes and equipment followed. Our wooden hut, quite large, had a sitting area, a bathroom, and two bedrooms, one with two beds and the other with three beds. It had to be John, Allan and me in one, and Mary and Antonia in the other. We all settled to sorting our things out and helping Mary with the outfits. We planned to shoot two pictures the next day. John went off for a reconnaissance with Gerry. We were tired and hungry. When John returned, we were asked to come to the mess hut and I will never forget the whoop that greeted us, from a room full of female-starved young men, yelling and cheering and crowding round us with beaming faces. They were so thrilled to have a diversion; a continuous stream of men came up to our table while we had supper. It became quite hot in there – hot food, hot men, and an ever-watchful Gerry.

We walked back to our quarters, escorted by our Mountie. I was feeling well fed and happy, and had forgotten the instant impact that being at the North Pole would have on our bodies the moment we stepped out of our shelters. It was extraordinary to walk out of the mess hut and to find it was still bright daylight, yet so intensely cold that every breath became a puff of white. It was very still and little warm glows came from the huts. Once we were back inside, after we had laboriously pulled off our boots and taken off our mittens and Parkas, we had a session to decide which outfit to start with. I laid out all the make-up on a table; John checked all his equipment with Allan; and Mary was busy sorting out her things. Excitement can be exhausting and bed soon called. We all slept with our vests, pyjamas, and socks on and it took a while to warm up. At around midnight, I was aware that John wasn't there, or indeed anywhere in the hut. I put on my Parka just to take a look outside and was alarmed to see him sitting on the ice, smoking a Gauloise. The light was weird. It seemed duller and greyer. There was no sound other than the low throb of the generator. Looking out on pure, clean ice and in bitterly cold air, it felt dangerous to stay out for too long. Bed again and a good sleep.

PG:

Now it was time to make pictures.

JK:

The next morning we had work to do. It was a great feeling. First, porridge for breakfast in the mess, then back to the hut to change. I put on the silk underwear and a sweater; then I started my make-up. First a moisturiser, followed by foundation; choosing one and adding a little of the other, I mixed them both in the palm of my hand. I fixed the resulting lotion with translucent powder. Then the eyes, carefully applying liquid eyeliner, then drawing this out on the upper lids. I added a creamy silver under the brows and some pencil under the eyes. It was a question of carefully building the look. Some blusher, very subtle, and scraped-back hair, pinned tight, and I was done. I put a chiffon scarf over my head to protect my make-up, took off the baggy sweater and put on a catsuit, then the boots, the coat, the hood, and the gloves. I was ready and we were off. I had to wear the Parka over the top and Gerry, pretty amazed but totally disciplined, helped me to totter to our special transport vehicle. Technically a Bombardier Snowmobile, it was like a Land Rover but bigger and with caterpillar tracks on the eight rear wheels. We all piled in and the American driver took us to our first location, barely twenty minutes from camp. The vehicle was lurching and bumping on the ice. It was very, very cold. Looking out, the landscape felt like a truly vast expanse; we were on the top of the world with seemingly limitless horizons. John indicated a place to stop. Gerry got out first and tested the ground. He then helped me out. Of course, I was wearing elegant boots and couldn't walk without slipping, so Gerry put me over his shoulder and carried me to the spot where John wanted me to pose.

I checked my face in a small hand-mirror. All was well. It was so incredibly cold but just about possible to hold a pose for a short time. Mary and Allan helped me to get settled. Then I sensed that the invisible string, connecting John and me, was in place. This is a powerful chemistry. It's as if nothing else matters, just the connection and our instinctive ability to get the image we need, working with total concentration and feeling it from the inside. My feet were turning to ice; a big hazard was the fact that the light was so strong I had to close

ARCTIC WHITE—ITS MAGNETIC DAZZLE reflected here in a white winter-evening cape with a pure snowfall of shape, a hood edged in white mink, helmet and gloves of silvery sequins. This, and the clothes on the next twelve pages, photographed in the silent brilliance of Resolute Bay, on Cornwallis Island in the Arctic Circle, where the unbelievable lighting from iceblinks and sunshifts changes the white of floes—and clothes—to shadowy mauve, blue, yellow. Cape by Ben Reig, of white silk faille, with a long princesse dress (unseen here) of the same fabric. Costume at Bonwit Teller; Dayton's; I. Magnin. Sequin gloves by Viola Weinberger; at Bergdorf Goodman. The sequin helmet by Adolfo.

JOHN COWAN

my eyes every few frames to protect them from the glare; Mary had to dab them as they then started to run. Also, I had to breathe in and hold my breath to avoid a cloud of white condensation spoiling the picture. We always knew when we had got the shot, and just as soon as we had it, I wrapped up again. We piled into the vehicle, huddled together and went back for hot soup. The next day promised to be great. We would be going by helicopter to a place with dramatic shapes and heights – spectacular natural ice sculptures. We prepared the outfit – silver sequin boots, gloves, and hood, which would shimmer in the highly reflective landscape, to accessorise and complement a regal, floor-length, heavy, creamy-white evening cape with a large, loose hood, trimmed in white mink.

I awoke the next morning after a wonderful cosy sleep in our hut and saw Mary in a yoga headstand. I joined her for ten minutes; then we all went out across the ice to the mess hut. The light was, as it always was, a strange, dull white. Steaming coffee and porridge in this cheerful and very male environment gave us fuel for our cold work. I spent time with the make-up; it had to be perfect as, of course, there were no make-up tables and mirrors to take out onto the ice. I dressed with thin layers of silk thermals, then a leotard, then the sequined top, silver tights, long sequined gloves and thin silver sequined boots; and finally the long and dramatic hooded cape. It was very heavy and the big hood – a triangular shape, wide and folding on the shoulders, buttoned under the chin – created a luxurious heart shape. The cape had slits for the hands, but my arm movements were restricted and this meant that I would have to be helped. We had a small helicopter with pilot for Gerry, Allan, John, and me. Mary checked me over, but stayed behind. With the big Parka around me, I clambered up, with difficulty, into the 'copter; then we were up and away, over the ice towards the ocean. Below, all was white as far as the eye could see, then some dark patches appeared in the distance. We headed towards what felt like the edge, then dropped down on to a patch near some ice that jutted out further, into the water.

John had his camera loaded and ready, knowing that freezing fingers and freezing metal would not be easy to work with. He looked round about with Gerry, then set up his tripod. The light was eerie, a greyish white. I was helped out of the helicopter and John directed us onto the jutting-out ice. I couldn't walk at all in the boots, slipping and sliding, so Gerry picked me up in a fireman's lift. With me on his shoulder, he prodded the ice and crossed a crack. Should I have been alarmed? He put me down on the spot John had pointed to. Once I was settled in place, I took it all in. We were actually on an ice floe. Gerry assured me it was safe. He had his metal spike, and was testing the ice. There were scary creaks and groans, apparently normal. The ice talked, the floe touching the ice mass. There were other flat floes, but this one had some magnificent heights, icicles and, incredibly, colours. The shadows seemed dark blue, green; the water, which had a stealthy current, was darker and deadly cold, not to be fallen into. We were ready and the concentration cranked up; our connection was tuned.

We took photographs. Having got here, in this awesome place, statuesque in this luxurious cape, I felt like a queen. John was so excited by the image. He felt, as did I, that we had got the picture after one roll of film. My feet turned into blocks of ice and I couldn't move my face. John said it was perfect; it felt perfect. We did shoot another roll, quickly for back-up. The floes, including the one we were on, were in fact moving. Before it became dangerous, Gerry, once again, scooped me over his shoulder like a sack of potatoes and calmly carried me back to safety. In a frozen daze, we clambered into the helicopter and headed back, knowing that we had something unique, feeling exhilarated as we thawed out.

A big hot bath, after help peeling off my outfit, was heaven. The few days left were filled with other photographs and some headshots – difficult, and also, I wondered, in such an awesome location, why do close-ups? I knew that we had the cracker, which was eventually printed double-page, as it deserved.

On our last night, the boys gave us a little show after supper and we females had a trail of guys requesting that we dance with them. One guy sought me out, insistently asking me to go to his hut for a surprise. I took John with me, as the mind boggled. What he showed us, as we walked in, was a cabin completely covered, every inch, with images – fashion, *Playboy* girls, funny cartoons, post cards. Blow me down, if he didn't have some pictures of me, taken from newspapers and magazines. When we flew away, back to normal life, I was in tears, hugging Gerry. I had such admiration for him. We could not have achieved the trip without his quiet strength and knowledge. What a man, out here in the wilds. He is the only Mountie I have ever met, but an unforgettable character in an unforgettable experience.

CONVALESCENCE: THE FIRST CAMERA TRY-OUT

Jill Kennington: **A day by the sea to find confidence again**

FOR NEARLY two months **Miss Jill Kennington,** the 22-year-old model, has been away from the cameras and the fashion salons. She was injured in a car crash. Her face was badly hurt. Now she is convalescing at her father's farm in Lincolnshire and preparing to get back to work. My picture is the first she has had taken since her crash. **John Cowan,** who took it, says: "It is important for a model whose face has been injured to recover her confidence before she can work again. We went to the coast near her home and took some pictures —just to ease her back into the thought of working again."

'Convalescence: the first camera try-out', by John Cowan, unsourced cutting, 1965

A setback

*an invitation to India – escape from the whirlwind of work –
time with family – the hand of fate – confidence takes a knock –
John proves very supportive*

PG:

*The Arctic trip generated stunning pictures. Then, the following year, you
went from one landscape extreme to another with the trips you made to Abu
Dhabi with John Cowan and then to Africa with Peter Beard for* Queen. *Tell
me about these.*

JK:

Well, first of all I was booked for a gorgeous trip to India for *Vogue* and
the British Wool Board, with Norman Parkinson. We were to go to
Kerala on the Malabar Coast, with all its inland waterways, where we
would be based on houseboats. But it was not to be. Fate intervened.
I was involved that winter in a serious car crash and was off work for
many weeks. It took me nearly fifty years to finally get to India.

PG:

Tell me about the car crash.

JK:

I went to Lincolnshire, for much needed feet-on-the-earth downtime
and home, with its wonderful, enveloping, comfortable hugs and
farmhouse cooking. My life felt like a whirlwind of energy and work
and I desperately needed the rest that Riby gave me. A long walk in
the clean fresh air with a few friends and the companionship of dogs.
My little beagle, Digby, who lived, or rather I plonked, in Riby was a
joy to me but a nightmare for my father. True to his deep-rooted pack
instincts, he was now escaping at night, rounding up any dogs he
could find or let out, in order to go hunting. It wasn't long before he
was banished to live with an uncle in the Isle of Wight. Digby became
very well known there, all around the island, as he did his rounds,
making friends. He had been given to me in a box, on a train going
up to Lincolnshire, by a beautiful young man called David, who I met
in Oxford. He was a truly sweet person and maybe this was his way of
trying to anchor me. However, London called instead.

On Sunday evening, after this particular weekend, I had to leave to
go back to work. I drove to Lincoln, then on to the A1. Fog started to
become hazardous and, by the time I was nearing Stamford, it had
become dangerously thick. I followed the car in front for quite some

miles, tricky now with no road signs - in fact the edge of the road was very hard to see. Suddenly the car in front braked and made as if to turn off onto the grass verge, leaving the clear view of headlights coming towards me. The A1 is an old Roman road, dead straight, except for one section where the lane I was in went left, while the straight part was for oncoming traffic only. Aaaggghhh! I slammed on my brakes, turning the wheel to also go over the grass but suddenly a car loomed behind me, coming fast, crashing into the back of my purple Mini. It propelled me straight into the oncoming car. Just before the crunch, I flung myself sideways, down onto the passenger seat, trying to avoid the windscreen glass. There was an almighty bang, a violent burst of white light in my head, a tumbling sensation; then nothing.

I must have lost consciousness for a while; and then I came to. A man's voice was saying, 'My God, is she dead?' Now I knew that I wasn't. I was numb before I started to feel the pain and then the awareness of a 'football' head. An ambulance arrived and I was carefully extracted, put on a stretcher, carried into the ambulance, and taken to Stamford infirmary. Once in the hospital, my body was becoming mine again, with this horrible pain in my head, arm, ribs, and pelvis. I thought that I had lost an eye; it felt like a wet balloon. I was assured that I was in one piece, albeit a broken one, and I thanked my lucky stars that I hadn't gone through the glass. My face had in fact bashed into the plastic record player, and the fact that it was gyroscopically mounted allowed it some give. The rest of my body hit the dashboard and steering wheel.

There were procedures. Summoning my strength, I had to give my name, parents' phone number, and anyone else's - of course, John's. He miraculously appeared as I came out of the X-ray department. I was very tearful and was told that I had to stay put. I was there for a good five days before I was discharged. I was then sent home, to be looked after at Church Farm, with an instruction to rest and to take the time needed to heal. John drove me there. My agent had to be told and the beautiful trip to India with Norman Parkinson sadly had to be cancelled, along with everything else. I took courage and decided to look in the bathroom mirror. It was a horrifying sight. My face was huge on one side; I could hardly see my red and swollen eye. Everything hurt. That side of my face was a jangle of painful nerves. When I breathed deeply, my chest hurt. I could only hobble back to lie down. I was fearful that this meant an end to my career as a model.

A trail of Lincolnshire friends came to see me, though I have to say, looking like this, I didn't want to see anyone. One friend was a trainee physiotherapist; she kept saying that she was sure something wasn't right. However, I had been discharged with no fractures, so I felt that I should just get on with life. John was a weekly visitor, much needed, and, after a few weeks, the swellings went down and he told me about a trip coming up for British *Vogue* – to Abu Dhabi. This was hugely exciting, but I had lost confidence. John took some test shots so that I could see myself – my face didn't look as bad as when I first scrutinised it in the mirror. I could do profile shots. So I made the commitment to go on the trip and what an extraordinary experience it was.

'Arabian Nights', by John Cowan, British, *Vogue*, July 1965

To Abu Dhabi with John Cowan

*guests of the Sheikh – palaces and a harem – land of falcons, horses,
and racing camels – bad news on returning to London*

PG:
So you were off once again, this time to Abu Dhabi.

JK:
I set off, not without some apprehension, John having gone first with
writer Polly Devlin to scout about. The plane stopped for a night in
Oman**.** I had a friend out there who was a Fleet Air Arm instructor.
He met me on my crutches and looked after me till my departure the
next day. I know that I still wasn't fully recovered, but some wonderful
experiences were had. We were the guests of Sheikh Shakhbut bin
Sultan, ruler of Abu Dhabi, and were made welcome in his palace.
An audience with the Sheikh was an unforgettable spectacle, with his
aides and falconers, sitting in a circle, in their beautiful robes and
headdresses. The falconers stroked their birds. We had tea in delicate
porcelain cups, were shown how to accept and how to politely decline
more, by rocking the cup from side to side. The Sheikh offered us
whatever help we needed and put his son, Said, at our disposal. We
learned much about Arabian culture and philosophy, including the
fact that no ruling Sheikh died a natural death, that when the time
came, an accident would happen. That was God's will.

Our plans involved making fashion pictures for British *Vogue*, and
also reportage images which John was to shoot for a separate feature
in the same issue.[1] Our hosts were very pleased to introduce us to
their country and its traditions. We spent time in the island capital
and, after a great feast given by Sheikh Said, we travelled in convoy
across the sands to the province of Buramai, governed by Sheikh
Shakhbut's brother Zayid. We spent four days there, staying in the
European guesthouse, set in the unexpected oasis of a green garden
with a swimming pool. It was all the stuff of dreams. On one excursion,
we met an English army officer, who was stationed at a small, old
fort – a strange place to be, surrounded by miles of desert. Then we
were introduced to the Sheikh's falcons, bred by an Englishman,

---

1 'Arabian Nights' and 'Flamman Allah, Abu Dhabi', July 1965

Roger Upton. We used one of these magnificent birds, which were all wearing splendid hoods, for a photograph. The falconers gave us a demonstration of flight and return, each handler having his own bird. We were also shown the Sheikh's Arab horses. I had a ride, but my hip hurt too much. Next, we met the racing camels, which I was taught to ride. This was easier on my pelvis, perhaps because your right knee is hooked round the pommel, of the saddle. I had a trot at a fast pace and a gallop - I felt like Lawrence of Arabia!

I recall a very privileged invitation. On our return from this amazing landscape of endless desert, the Sheikh invited us girls to visit his wives. They lived in their own guarded palace. We were taken by personal staff, dressed in wafting white robes, into an exotic room filled with silk cushions. It was huge, with palatial arches that let in the light, yet the room was cool. In the centre of this space was a low table laden with sweet pastries, dates, and fruit; and once again we sat in a circle. There were thirteen wives, the youngest being about thirteen and the eldest about forty. They appeared to be very close and affectionate. I can't describe their faces, as they all wore leather masks with almond-shaped slits for the eyes, which were blackened with kohl. The leather came down the middle of the face, covering the nose. The women would raise this in order to eat and to drink tea out of delicate cups. This all made quite a bizarre impression, on the one hand of riches, evident in the setting and coloured silk clothes, and on the other this basic mask. It reminded me of the falcons' hoods. I smiled as we were introduced one by one. Some sat politely; some giggled; and when they were more relaxed, after much studying, they asked if they could touch my hair and hands. Their hands, in contrast to my pale skin, were covered in henna designs. It was a wonderful trip and in such contrast to the modern city that Abu Dhabi has become.

PG:
What opportunities, unimaginable today. Then back to London.

JK:
And to unexpected complications. When I got back to England, I went to my dentist. With daily pain in my face, I thought I might have a tooth problem. I had just started to open my mouth, when he said, 'Jill, there is something seriously wrong here. I am going to take you to the London Clinic.' In short, I had a fractured skull and a flattened cheekbone, as well as a fractured pelvis and broken ribs. So I saw a specialist surgeon and, with the help of photographs, I had an operation to rebuild the cheekbone. Amazingly, my recovery was fast, aided by the surgeon's skill and my youth. Soon I was ready to face the world - and ready for more adventures in foreign lands.

Brilliantly flowering peignoir,
opposite, in featherweight
Terylene lawn. By Angela Gore,
£7 12s. 6d., at Fiona;
other shops, last page.
Desert flying, wildly flowering
voile, *this page*. Bra, shorts,
and skirt to wrap round.
17 gns., to order at Daphne Hughes.
Printed voile by Liberty.
Lipsticks: Charles of the Ritz
new Basic Pink, *opposite*,
and Sunny Red, *this page*.
Dream location—no mirage—
real desert country,
everywhere sun, sand, silence:
Buramai, a huge oasis
in the heart of Arabia, encircled
by tiny villages, gardens
and trees—and rivers giving
Buramai a natural water supply,
a dream come true for desert travellers

'Arabian Nights', by John Cowan, British, *Vogue*, July 1965

Jill with Kandy, by Peter Beard, 1965

To Kenya with Peter Beard

to Karen Blixen's Africa for Queen *- Veruschka -*
land of huge skies and red dust, beautiful people, and magnificent wildlife
- evenings around the camp fire - shooting fashion on safari -
Africa under the skin

PG:
And very soon after Abu Dhabi you were off to Kenya. Tell me about that trip.

JK:
Life certainly was a whirlwind of exciting work - the agency had to turn down so much. But I stuck to my guns about just doing interesting shoots with good photographers. One day I was booked with David Montgomery, in his Edith Grove studio. We were doing a job for *Queen*. Clare Rendlesham was the fashion editor. Anyway, as I got ready for the last picture, Clare whispered to me that she wanted to talk to me about something after we had finished. She had a glint in her eye. I touched up my blusher, dishevelled my hair, which was big and romantic, and got into the atmosphere, trying to think beautiful. Then, job done, I got into my own clothes, took off my eyelashes, cleaned my face ... and waited for Clare. She came into the dressing room in her suit with miniskirt and boots, pulled the door shut behind her, and asked, 'Would you like to do a spread in Africa?' My heart skipped a beat. 'Africa?' 'Yes, Kenya.' I had only ever read about the flavour of Kenya, in Elspeth Huxley's *The Flame Trees of Thika*. 'Who is the photographer?' 'Peter Beard.'[1]

I had already met Peter in New York, where we had done some photographs with Giacometti sculptures. Apparently, he had specifically asked for me on this job, and also the aristocratic German model Vera von Lehndorff, known simply as Veruschka. I had also met Veruschka in New York and had seen her work. I was thrilled to be asked and agreed instantly, though I had a few anxieties about not being six-foot tall and wondered if I would be able to carry off any photographs with her. Would I be able to hold my own? Clare said that I definitely would. Then there was a flurry of information, checking of dates, and this amazing opportunity became a reality - Clare and I were flying to Nairobi, with suitcases full of clothes.

---

1 'In Africa', November 3rd 1965

Peter had arranged to be at the airport to meet us. As we landed, I could see him sitting on the roof of the very small arrivals building, legs over the side, in his usual gear of shirt, shorts, and sandals. It was great to see him again. He whisked us through passport control; we were waved through customs; and out we went into the heat accompanied by a cool breeze. Vehicles were ready to transport us to the centre of Nairobi and the New Stanley Hotel.

On arrival at the hotel, we dispersed to check in, with an agreement to meet up for a plan-of-action discussion in the famous courtyard café of the hotel, the tables shaded by a big thorn tree. We gathered and had drinks and a sandwich, as Peter unfolded his plans – music to my enraptured ears. We were to stay in Nairobi for twenty-four hours, rest up overnight, get anything we needed, and the next day we were invited to have lunch with Jack Block, who owned the New Stanley and the older Norfolk Hotel. He was an influential man, who had kindly put us up in return for an acknowledgement in the *Queen* feature. I desperately wanted to acquire a bush jacket, which Peter helped me to find, not letting me go on my own in the streets of Nairobi, which were full of buzz and bustle and smells of spice, the men and women of Kenya all going about their business. We passed colourful markets, with many fruits and vegetables that I didn't recognise, until we came to an army surplus shop with second-hand kit, including racks of jackets. I quickly found one, put it on, and felt very happy.

The next day, Jack Block's sumptuous house, with a pool in the garden, was filled with the local well-to-do, curious about us and our plans. Veruschka had arrived, so our party was complete. It was Sunday and a huge curry banquet was laid out, apparently a tradition. I couldn't wait to go into the bush. The following day, we set off in two Land Rovers – with Peter's trusted tracker, Gula Gula, drivers, luggage, and cameras – and headed for Tsavo national park, to stay with the game warden, David Sheldrick, and his wife, Daphne. The road gradually became a dust track and I truly felt that we were in Africa – red dust, thorn trees, and the occasional baobab, so crazy and beautiful. We arrived at the ranch, the main house and other buildings all spread out and surrounded by stunning tropical gardens, which meandered into the distance, and on into the bush. David and Daphne were so charming; this was very old-fashioned English living, in Africa (I had read by now, ahead of the trip, Karen Blixen's *Out of Africa*). Their capable trustworthiness and knowledge of wildlife, and the responsibility of running a park, this being the largest, were impressive. Daphne rescued orphaned elephants and I went to visit the latest arrival, a baby still covered all over with soft hair and with a floppy little trunk, whose mother had been shot by poachers, I fed it from a bottle and fell in love.

We departed the Sheldricks and went on our way again for a few hours, in our two Land Rovers. It was a rough ride but great to be rattling around on our way to the camp of conservationist Glen Cotter. The African skies were huge and endless, and we had our first significant sighting of wildlife: a huge herd of zebra, then impala, and some ostriches, which took off at a lick, seemingly running at the same speed as us. I couldn't wait to work in this landscape. We arrived at Glen's camp, very rustic and simple: a big tent each and one as wardrobe, and a shower that consisted of a bucket and hosepipe with an up-to-the-neck tarpaulin around it. Lunch, made by the African cooks, was waiting for us in the big mess tent, where we talked about the first pictures. After lunch, I made up, as natural a look as possible, and put on a long, soft, thin Irish wool skirt and matching shirt with a wide belt. Gentle to start with, the first shoot was conceived as a sort of 'walking on the plains' picture, with zebra dotted about, so we took off to find a herd. Feet on the earth and aware of our surroundings, Peter and I walked and shot pictures. Veruschka took her turn while I changed into a bright green suit and pale knee boots, to be shot with a magnificent mature baobab tree as the backdrop. The light mellowed and became softer. The baobab was close by. Peter seemed to know every inch of the area. Because the tree was so big, I had to lean forward, so that we could get it all in the frame with a wide-angle lens and avoid distortion. I put my hands out, fingers stretched, in case I fell. This was the pose that Peter captured. The first day, and we already had some pictures under our belt.

PG:

It sounds like you were well on your way to a great feature.

JK:

Yes, and that evening we could relax. The situation was magical, sitting around a fire, with the smells of cooking and night sounds in the background. We talked about tomorrow, about catching rhino and making photographs while this was happening. It all sounded a bit hair-raising. Glen was one of the first conservationists to capture rhino. After a period of settling down in a special corral, they would be transported by the crew and released into an area low on rhino. This is common practice now, but not then. The prospect was exciting, to be sure, and we turned in for an early start, having decided what the outfits would be. I liked Veruschka very much and we were at ease with each other. Peter settled down, stretched out on his tummy on the earth, to write in his diary. Clare was content. I drifted off to sleep knowing that guards were keeping the fire burning and any animals away. The next day's shoot went according to plan; the rhino was safely caught and secured; we worked around this to get some great pictures.

The northern part of Tsavo National Park covers about 2,500 square miles of wild semi-arid country. You can stay here in Glen Cottar's camp, on the north bank of the Athi River. The suit is in ribbed silk, battle-dress shape, with high revers, tabbed and buckled at waist and cuffs. By Susan Small. Beige cotton boots with patent toes, by Capezio for Rayne. Shops are on page 158

86

'In Africa', by Peter Beard, *Queen*, November 3rd 1965

That evening, after supper with pili pili ho ho sauce, made with amazingly hot chilli – the 'ho ho' name came about out of necessity, the sound made when cooling one's mouth – Veruschka gave me a haircut, lopping off an inch in length. Round the campfire, companionship was close and we were a happy party. Gula Gula, Peter's tracker, was with us, sitting quietly, taking us in. Of course we talked about the following day's photographs. It was to be a beachwear shoot. Veruschka and I were to paint ourselves black. Peter chose a hippo mud pool as the location. The night sounds were so special, different from the morning chorus, which came all too soon. We were up at 6.00am, and after a breakfast of porridge, Veruschka and I got to grips with sponges and Leichner body-black. The reason local Masai girls weren't used for the shoot was because it would have been too complicated to ask the elders to give their permission and then to wait for meetings to be held. The stage make-up was surprisingly easy to apply and we were able to do it without making streaks. It seemed to go into the pores and the result gave our skin a sheen. By the time we had scraped our damp hair back into a knot, we looked fantastic.

We dressed carefully, and then, sitting on towels, we drove to the hippo pool. Hippos were there but messing about, with lots of snorting, and they were somewhat excited. Peter felt it wasn't safe to stand there, with our backs to them, as there was a baby in the group. So we moved off into the open, did some touching up with the body-black, and settled into making a picture of the two of us together. Veruschka and I worked the photograph as a team, in the same way, and it felt good. Well, I suppose this was a first, blackening white skin, before black models made their way into all-white magazines. It was a labour to get the make-up off, with lots of soap and scrubbing under the open-top shower until my skin was sore, but it came off eventually.

Thinking of this, I am reminded that I worked the following year for *Elle* in Saint-Tropez with Ronald Traeger, and the stunning Donyale Luna, probably the first highly visible black model.[2] She came over from New York and worked a lot in Europe after that shoot, becoming well known for her striking, exotic look.

PG:
This trip certainly sounds more like a safari adventure than a conventional fashion shoot.

---

2 'La magie des nuits d'été', July 7th 1966

'In Africa', Jill and Veruschka, by Peter Beard, *Queen*, November 3rd 1965

JK:

With *Queen* we enjoyed such editorial freedom. We could really tell a story and take chances. Inviting Peter to create these pictures was an inspired choice. He had a unique vision; for him the clothes, the fashion element, were incidental. He was in his element playing off two striking models against the vistas that he loved and understood so well. Our African days were a dream – waking to unfamiliar sounds, space, huge skies revealing red and purple dawns, the Swahili chatter of the cooks, and the wafting aromas of breakfast. Our work took us to a Masai Mara camp. Peter chatted up the young warriors with the help of Gula Gula. A strong smell of blood and milk, which is the Masai diet, emanated from the camp and from their skin. A wonderful double shot was achieved with a tall, stick-thin but strong young man between us holding a spear, so proud looking. Next we tracked a leopard. Peter photographed it on the branch of a tree, resting. He then shot a view of me under the tree, standing on the roof of the Land Rover in a leopard coat. Peter and the magazine's art department were able to merge the photographs together. I hasten to add that times and perceptions, mine included, have changed and the leopard coat and certain other things we didn't question then would be seen from different perspectives today.

We went to Mount Kenya, where we stayed with 'Wildlife Billy', Bill Woodley, the game warden. He had an orphaned baby lion, which I held and bottle-fed. Having climbed up the mountain peaks, we slept in the open before taking pictures the next day with giant lobelia. This whole trip had such magic. I know it couldn't have been achieved with anyone but Peter. He spent six months of the year in Kenya, where he was completely at one with nature – his knowledge of game was vast. He seemed to know everyone who had settled and made their life in Kenya. Peter was very handsome, with a flop of sun-kissed hair. He was always dressed in the same shorts, shirt, and sandals; his possessions were a camera and a diary; and he cut a dishevelled but dashing figure. His courage was huge, he seemed fearless. He would spot a herd of elephants, stop the Land Rover, and take off into the bush to investigate. He made a beautiful study of crocodiles, which became a book called *Eyelids of Morning*, and made another book on elephants. There were heart-rending pictures of the consequences of poachers' crimes and of the effects of drought. Tragically, so many elephants died. Peter's work needed a lot of time and commitment, which he gave. The trip was fantastic. It was great to work with Peter and there were some precious times talking round the campfire at the end of the day. Africa got under my skin and into to my heart. When we left, I suffered from *mal d'Afrique*, and still do.

The end of a chapter

*an intense partnership, personal and professional,
comes under pressure – betrayal –
A pox on both your houses*

PG:
Jill, it seems that, by this time, you were in constant demand, working and travelling non-stop – with John, but also with other photographers. How did this impact on your working and personal relationship with John?

JK:
There were many, many trips and jobs that I had to say no to, as it was physically impossible. I did seem to be in constant demand, which was great. I always found it painful to miss something good. I was determined to work with other great photographers, which clearly frustrated John. It often happened that a shoot for John was conditional upon me being the model, so a job would sometimes collapse when the client learned I wasn't free.

PG:
But you still worked with John?

JK:
Yes, and we did some great pictures, but I managed my own schedule and accepted only the jobs with John that sounded interesting. Sometimes it was a case of squeezing in a shoot with John between my other commitments – like the time we managed to fit in a job in Paris that involved working at night in an already busy schedule; but the job had seemed promising and turned out to be very exciting from a fashion perspective. The shoot was for *Petticoat*,[1] a teen magazine and not my usual territory. The fashion editor was Liz Smith, who was very smart – she went on to work for the *Observer* magazine – and I understood I would be modelling creations by a sensational designer.

PG:
Tell me more.

JK:
It was Paris; it was the Collections; and it was in a studio that we had worked in before for *Elle*, off Saint-Honoré, near the wonderful

---

1 'Clothes that click', April 2nd 1966

delicatessen Fauchon, so great for picking up supper. The Collections shoots were often at night, after the shows held during the day. Things were highly organised. Clothes would appear, pre-booked, for the magazine or newspaper that had organised this from London or New York or elsewhere. This created an atmosphere of anticipation and of secrecy as we could not talk about who was designing what until after publication. The clothes I was to model were from the inaugural haute-couture collection by Paco Rabanne. This became the moment that he exploded onto the fashion scene as an amazing innovative talent.

A courier arrived with an assistant, clothes on soft-padded hangers, reams of protective tissue paper. Removing this revealed extra-ordinary, never-seen-before garments constructed from linked wafer-slender coloured plastic discs or small reflective metal rectangles that shimmered in the light. Rabanne's ideas were a radical statement of modernity. These were very provocative designs that demanded poses to match. The shots, against a black background, were simple but striking. I remember the first time that I *heard* the clothes – the tinkling sounds when I walked across the backdrop.

PG:
It sounds like your feet never touched the ground.

JK:
So yes, John and I still shared these experiences, but I felt increasingly constricted by the pressures he exerted on me. There was a time when he tried very hard to persuade me that he could be my agent. He had set up a model agency, Agency 39, which he ran briefly from the studio; and, of course, he wanted me on his books. But I shied away from this as it felt like he wanted to take ownership of me. I also discovered that, for test shots, John would raid my personal wardrobe for clothes in which to dress the girl. Not good. By nature, I am generous, but I do like to be asked.

There were social things that I sadly missed out on when away on jobs, like the Women of the Year lunch in a big London hotel, parties, friends getting married, and other events; and I was so busy that I had to decline attractive work opportunities too, including some great American *Vogue* trips that I was offered. Bookings came in sometimes three months ahead. I can't remember ever going on holiday. My breaks came at weekends when I wasn't away – and I would spend them in London with friends, or in the country; and there were also visits to Lincolnshire, where I felt grounded. I remember feeling as if piranha fish were taking pieces of me, people were always wanting me,

'Clothes that click', by John Cowan, *Petticoat*, April 2nd 1966

socially and in the work context – and John in particular. Nonetheless, I thought – wrongly as it happened – that he and I were together for the long haul. Yet my trust in him wavered at times, instilling in me a feeling of insecurity. I suspected that sometimes he had a fling with another woman when I was away. It was purely instinct, but I was proved right in due course. I came back to Princes Place one day to find John sitting in the studio with a small-time actress on his knee. She looked at me in the most amazingly defiant way, her eyes telling me that she had had my man.

I loved John, but I needed to trust him. The loss of trust meant the end of our relationship. Sadly for John, after we split, I don't think he ever found another girl with whom he had the terrific rapport and working creativity that was unique to us.

PG:
So, an intense working and personal partnership came to an end in 1966. Wasn't there a short film John made with you, towards the end of your relationship? Did it reflect elements of your lives? What is the backstory to that film?

JK:
There were a few occasions when John showed an interest in film. The first event he filmed was a press show of Mary Quant's clothes, her first in Paris. It was held at the smart Hôtel Crillon. I took part in it and, as usual with Mary, it was good fun, very different to the haute couture feel, very much alive and young. I remember how much Paris – amazingly – loved what was happening in London, and how much the magazine journalists clamoured and fussed, especially those from *Elle*, *Jardin des Modes*, *Marie Claire*, and *Paris Match*, and also those in Paris for American titles such as *Women's Wear Daily* and *Life*. The film, as far as I recall, gave a good impression of the show.

The next film that John made was a short, involving myself with Ray Davies and The Kinks, which was a spoof. We spent a lot of time messing around and being silly. It was funny and tender, with of course Kinks music; but now no one seems able to find it or know what has happened to it. I hope it isn't in a shed at the bottom of a garden somewhere, gathering dust and damp, but I fear it is lost forever.

One little 16mm film, the one you refer to, has survived. Over many weekends in the last year of our relationship, John would suggest that we take off somewhere and shoot some footage. We went to the sand dunes near Rye and up to my parents' farm in Lincolnshire.

I don't think there was any direction really; it was just about being free, just being. There are great shots in wide, open landscapes and fun sequences of me larking around with the farm animals, driving a tractor, and so on. After we split up, John filmed his assistant Richard Dawkins at night in London, then put the two parts together, cutting between day and night, two different moods, one joyful, one melancholic, overlaying this with very moody music and a voice speaking Richard's thoughts, a narrative of his doomed relationships.

It wasn't until after John died that I saw this; he had given the reel to my mother and, amazingly, she had it safe in a box. I had, by the way, done a documentary with Anglia Television the year before, which was great, shot on the sands near Cleethorpes, on the farm, and riding through woods, with a voice-over of thoughts. Maddeningly, this seems to have disappeared. I wonder where this filming would have led us, if we had carried on; but maybe there is something special about a moment in time that can never be snatched back. Well, John's film certainly expressed what was in his head – me being free, the man sombre and unhappy. I do think it depicts how he felt when we broke up – dark, dark, brooding. And he gave it the ghastly but pointed title of *A pox on both your houses*. There are some sequences that I am very happy with, for example the atmosphere around home, Church Farm; but there are scenes that are really not me. John had a thing about guns and target shooting – he would fire a gun from the studio mezzanine across to a target on the opposite wall, where a propped-up mattress would absorb the shock. Crazy. But it was not my taste to fire a weapon; nor was blowing smoke at a parrot, which I felt was cruel. However, there it was, the bitter-sweet finale to my intense, roller-coaster, often fraught, but creative and hugely productive relationship with John Cowan.

Waiting for Antonioni

WHEN part of swinging London, in the person of **John Cowan**, the photographer, moved in to take over part of dismal W.11, only a handful of Notting Hill folk took any notice. But now, as my picture shows, things are really looking bright in the Cowan quarter.

What's happened is that Cowan himself has been taken over. **Michelangelo Antonioni**, the Italian film director, is making a feature film which takes in all of the photographer's studios and nearly all his models.

Leading ladies of the model world like **Jill Kennington**, 23 ; **Melanie Hampshire**, 22 ; **Peggy Moffitt**, 26 ; and **Rosaline Murray** have spent all week on practice parade before the moving cameras.

The photographer is played by an actor. So Mr. Cowan is banished with his two secretaries and his large dog to a caravan in the street outside. Even his flat above the studios is playing a part in the film.

Signor Antonioni and his unit have been at work there six weeks. Mr. Cowan is, naturally, not being put to this inconvenience for nothing.

The film men have based their production unit in a betting shop opposite the studio. The publicity manager has, with fine humour, been given an office in the corner pub.

Spokesman

THE Household Brigade has chosen a successor to Major Iain Erskine as their public relations officer. He is Major **Peter de Zulueta**, 38, son-in-law of novelist **Daphne du Maurier.**

Major de Zulueta, an extra equerry for two years to Prince Philip, left the Welsh Guards

PICTURE BY MICHAEL McKEOWN

Leading ladies in W.11 : Left to right, Rosaline Murray, Melanie Hampshire, Peggy Moffitt, Jill Kennington

'Waiting for Antonioni', Rosaleen Murray, Melanie Hampshire, Peggy Moffitt, and Jill, by Michael McKeown, unsourced cutting, 1966

Cast for Antonioni's
Blow-Up

*the Italian director plans a film to be set in London –
the central character is a fashion photographer – Veruschka as herself –
Princes Place becomes a key location – the fashion shoot – the contrasts
between being a model and acting the role of a model*

PG:

*Jill, 1966 was the year of your break-up with John. It was also the year in
which you were cast for a role in Michelangelo Antonioni's* Blow-Up *and
created an indelible image that has become emblematic of the London scene
in the Sixties. How did this happen?*

JK:

I remember these excited whispers going round London: 'Antonioni
is going to make a movie here!' He was very well known to me for
his beautiful and often strange films, so I was intrigued, but it took
a while to understand that he was interested in the London scene,
in particular the world of fashion photographers and models. The
film unfolds over the course of twenty-four hours and revolves
around the mystery of a murder that the central character, a fashion
photographer, believes he has unwittingly captured on film. *Blow-Up*
is often best remembered for its depiction of the fashionable milieu
in which it is set; and clearly Antonioni wanted to get this right and
did a lot of research. I sometimes saw him sort of skulking around, not
wanting to be noticed, alone, just taking it all in – both in the trendy
discotheques and in my favourite Italian restaurant, San Lorenzo. He
sent questionnaires to a number of photographers, hoping that their
answers would help him build an authentic picture of a successful
young fashion photographer. I know that John had one, and the
location people came to see his studio. One day, Antonioni turned up
on a shoot I was doing at David Montgomery's Edith Grove studio for
Harper's Bazaar.[1] This became the template for the fashion shoot in
the film and defined the part I would eventually play, though it didn't
reflect my preferred, animated way of working.

At the Montgomery shoot, I remember there were two other girls –
Melanie Hampshire and Peggy Moffitt. We were introduced, told that

---

1 'Bazaar's summer fashion launch', May 1966

Antonioni was just going to watch and to ignore him. This was very easy as he just faded away to a grey figure, alone at the back of the studio, like a ghost in the shadows, observing. I was a bit disappointed that the shoot was quite abstract and still and not typical of my type of work. The pictures were highly stylised, the three of us striking poses with large sheets of thin transparent plastic and making shapes that would catch the light and add a graphic element. I am quite sure that seeing this shoot inspired and influenced Antonioni's decision to pose the models in the film like inanimate mannequins between translucent panels; but I would emphasise that his view was not my reality. That said, I found myself in a kind of unplanned audition. The three of us were cast for the film after his close observation of the Montgomery shoot. Of course, only when the filming started, with five girls in a similarly static, stylised studio set, could I see how that shoot had given him ideas.

PG:

John Cowan's studio became the principal set for Blow-Up. *How did his style of working relate to the photographer in the film?*

JK:

The scene with David Hemmings as the photographer and Veruschka as herself was pure Cowan. Antonioni must have seen him working – and I never saw anyone else take pictures quite that way. The shooting on the floor – downwards, completely fluid, un-hindered by tripods or anything else – was typical Cowan, though I am sure for the movie there were also influences from other photographers, for other scenes. I should add that Veruschka was the only person who could have played the scene like that. I imagine that she may have been asked to end up on the floor, but who knows; it was a happening, and brilliant. I would have loved to have a one-on-one scene like that, but Antonioni had never witnessed me at work in my usual way, and it was not to be.

I think that the Hemmings character has some Bailey traits. Bailey, as a contract photographer for *Vogue* and with the considerable publicity that he provoked, was the most prominent of the new younger talents. *Blow-Up* certainly captured the essence of London photographers in the Sixties. It was as if a page had turned, and the character in the film became a blend of various personalities that represented the new generation.

I don't know all the studios Antonioni visited, but John Cowan's and David Montgomery's were certainly two. There are suggestions of the liveliness of Brian Duffy, the attention to detail of Terry Donovan,

'Bazaar's summer fashion launch', by David Montgomery,
British *Harper's Bazaar*, May 1966

of David Bailey, and of laid-back and quiet David Montgomery. The two that I see most in the Hemmings character, though, are Bailey and Cowan – Bailey because he could be cheeky and often rude, but still appealing; Cowan because of the way he dressed, and the way he worked. His body language, his fluidity, and the way the camera became a part of him are so like Hemmings's interpretation of the role.

Terence Donovan might also have been the inspiration for some specific details. He drove around in a Rolls-Royce, usually in jeans and an open-necked shirt. At weekends, he was out and about, going to markets and antique shops and generally on the look-out. Antonioni copied this for the Hemmings character. I remember being in Terry's Rolls one weekend, feeling wonderfully liberated, with the purr of the powerful engine and the luxurious smell of leather, speeding through the quiet London streets. Nothing like it is today.

PG:
And the studio?

JK:
John's studio in Princes Place became 'the studio'. It was perfect because it was very big, a really cavernous space, and there were large double doors onto the street, making it possible for vehicles and huge equipment to be driven in. Antonioni made some modifications to suit his needs, for example adding the walkway that connected the mezzanine living area to the darkroom on that same upper level, which was installed specially for the film.

John had an old wood propeller in his studio. My photographer friend and John's former assistant, Richard Dawkins, recently reminded me of this and that its home was in the gallery space, which overlooked the studio below. John had a wonderful graphic eye and this propeller reflected his sense of shape and drama. I don't know if it was ever used for one of his photographs – no pictures spring to mind – but of course it is tempting to connect this with the scene in which the film's fictional photographer purchases a propeller in an antiques shop.

The hiring of the studio by the film company saved John once again from the bailiffs. When the film company moved in, he cleared out to a caravan parked in the street outside the studio. John, by the way, also made some extra money by renting the Land Rover that features in certain scenes to the production company.

PG:

Fascinating. So there clearly were details that Antonioni picked up from John Cowan and others to add authenticity to the character. And we also see a number of his pictures of you in the studio.

JK:

Yes, there were big exhibition prints, blow-ups of shots we had done together. The picture of me on the Temple Griffin in a black leather coat, from the series posed on major London monuments for *Queen*, appears fleetingly in the film. The one of me dangling from the parachute is more visible; you can see this clearly behind David Hemmings during the fashion shoot scene. These images are dynamic and very different from the film's fashion shoot. They show how I had really found my natural style through working with John. What you see on the walls of the studio in *Blow-Up*, were typical Kennington/Cowan location shots. It was weird, to say the least, when I discovered what I was being asked to do in *Blow-Up*. I remember thinking that I shouldn't do it, that I was being unfair to myself, that I was to be an under-used, bit-part player. But I then turned the thoughts around and told myself, 'This is Antonioni; it is his vision; and the whole thing is a bit of a mystery.' Now that the film is such a cult classic, I am really glad that I did it. We were pieces in an artist's jigsaw puzzle.

The scenes that I was in were static, and very abstract. Actually, I really like that now. I can see that Antonioni needed some stillness; it slows things down; a real contrast to Veruschka's scene. Our fashion scene was his creation, an impression rather than a precise reconstruction of reality. The five girls, graphically positioned, in bold clothes and make-up, looked very good. At the time, I hated the fact that we appeared so doll-like. The fact that we had to play it dumb didn't appeal to me. I often felt that there was a lot to defend. Okay, some models may be dumb, but I am not one of them. Here I was doing precisely that, playing a vacuous creature. In real life, I never experienced anything other than respect and enthusiasm. But this was a movie and I was playing a part. The film created its own reality and, by the end, do we really know what it is about? I think Antonioni loved to play with our perceptions, our psyche, and to leave us questioning.

PG:

Jill, it is interesting to realise that, for so many of us, the film – a work of fiction – came to define the realities of that world. How true did you consider David Hemmings's interpretation of the role of the photographer?

Jill and Peggy Moffitt, by Arthur Evans, 1966

JK:

I thought David Hemmings was terrific. He was physically slight, more like David Bailey, but the way he worked in the film had the charisma of John Cowan. When we started shooting, I don't know what sort of research, if any, he did, but he just nailed the role. He was so perfectly cast, an appealing bundle of energy and of course he was very young and attractive. There was no arrogance; he was just a member of the team. The actual shooting of *Blow-Up* was more fun than you might expect. David used to hang out with us girls over in the dressing room, chatting while we did our hair and make-up. This was a good move, as he got to know us and we all felt at ease with him. We then dressed and walked over to the studio. It was all somewhat surreal. David's body language and natural familiarity with a camera were convincing. He would run on the spot and do deep breathing exercises before a take to raise his adrenaline levels, and he certainly gave the impression he really was a photographer, not just playing the role.

Antonioni arranged us, then told us to just stand there. Lights and sound were checked and then David appeared. In a genuine shoot there is always a rapport, a connection between photographer and model; but here there was none. As it was, we gave the impression of being totally controlled. For the fashion tableau, I stood, inanimate, with the other girls in a receding diagonal between the translucent panels. My bold blue and white stripy top and hat looked great, but I couldn't move, which was part of the plan – the outfit had been designed for effect rather than to be wearable. The hat was an important part of it, made by James Wedge, the trendy milliner. He reminded me that he was instructed to exaggerate the look and the hats certainly gave the outfits more pizzazz. Although I felt rigid, the end result was eye-catching, and I was on the poster for the film in France, a collage of myself and the famous image of David with Veruschka. The evening outfit, a long chiffon dress, was easier to wear. I remember asking for a wind-machine for a solo shot taken by Arthur Evans, the stills photographer, which gave it some life. But that was not in line with Antonioni's vision and I don't believe the shot was ever used.

I am pleased to have had the opportunity to work for Antonioni – and to see him at work. He was a very attractive man, with a slim build and wavy, slightly greying hair, a lined face, quiet eyes and a slow smile; many, possibly sad, experiences were expressed in his demeanour. He was immensely likeable and sensitive and with an air of mystery about him. I warmed to him, but he was a man who kept his distance. In the studio he was in charge, but a voyeur; and in his own time he was very private. It must be an enormous job creating a film that is as you have visualised it in your head. He was extremely talented and in Italy he wasn't simply Michelangelo Antonioni, he was the 'Maestro'.

Career-wise, *Blow-Up* was different and it was exciting. Now, with hindsight, I am even more pleased to have been a part of it. It is fun that so many young people have seen it and really appreciate it; and, curiously, and significantly, it is unique in that it took a maestro from another country to realise that a slice of Sixties London was worth recording, even though his interpretation took on the character of a mystery, a fantasy, or an illusion. Sometimes people ask me what *Blow-Up* was about. I haven't a clue. But it is unforgettable.

Jill, by Arthur Evans, 1966

Changes and challenges

a new relationship – living in Paris – advice from Ronald Traeger –
a traumatic trip to Ireland – a family tragedy – the Paris riots in 1968 –
work provides an escape from domestic challenges

PG:
Jill, 1966 saw you cast in Blow-Up, *a memorable career moment, but also marked the split from John. What came next?*

JK:
I hadn't realised how traumatised I would feel, breaking up with John. I knew it was right and that my trust in him was broken, but, nevertheless, I had a big hole in my inner self. I found, with the help of a friend, a pretty garden flat in Earl's Court Square. It felt like a safe place. I saw good friends when I wasn't working, one in particular, called Anthony, who was incredibly funny, so I laughed a lot, which was good therapy. He was a great support through that time. I remember, a little later, in 1968, my laughing friend taking me to the premiere of the Barbra Streisand film *Funny Girl*. It was a glamorous red-carpet do, followed by dinner. And of course work kept me busy and focused.

One day my booker, Jill took off with a man – to Greece, I think it was – and never came back. David Puttnam, who was then an advertising whizz, had set up a select stable of about six photographers, an agency of talent; he also represented Richard Avedon in London. I had already worked for Avedon in London, doing a super-cool advertising head shot, with only my eyes visible through a white 'space-age' helmet and holding up a shoe in my silver-gloved hand.[1] The shoot was in David Montgomery's studio. Learning that my booker had gone, David Puttnam asked me to join his agency as the only model, which I did. Work was going well and the most difficult part was fending off offers. London was buzzing, with new young talent arriving from Paris and New York. The city was in its stride, influencing style worldwide. I was always busy, working and making the most of life.

I met this man – let's call him Mr X – very soon after the split from John. He had manipulated a meeting, as I later discovered, through a girlfriend, Marie-Lise. He was insanely attractive, worked in movies – he had been involved with *Doctor Zhivago* – and drove a Maserati. By curious coincidence, I had attended the premiere of *Doctor Zhivago*,

---

1   British *Vogue*, April 15th 1966; *Queen*, April 27th 1966

in 1966, and I had done photographs on the Moscow street set for *Queen*. But our paths had not yet crossed. Unplanned, as life often is, a whirlwind romance started. He seemed to want all my time. We went to the theatre, ate in the Trattoria Terrazzo in Soho, went clubbing, and he came home to Lincolnshire. I went to New York on a work trip with *Harper's Bazaar*, staying on for other things that Eileen Ford had arranged. Mr X came out and we stayed at the Fords' place on Long Island.

When I returned, I had work in Paris with Helmut for *Elle*, for an extended feature. I loved working with Helmut. We did a trip to Brittany, which was full of paths through wildflower meadows, windmills, and seascapes, staying in a lovely, small, rustic farmhouse hotel with delicious food and log fires. On my return to London, I had a meeting with Puttnam and Avedon to discuss an advertising campaign for Clairol. I remember we met in a hotel at the end of Jermyn Street. I had enjoyed working with Avedon before and had such respect for him. This was a serious request and I would have loved the opportunity to work with him again on a prestigious campaign, but I would have to let Clairol dye my hair solid blonde. I had a big problem with this, as for years I had carefully had a few fine highlights put in by the genius Daniel Galvin. My hair had a beautiful, natural, child-in-the-sun look and solid blonde wasn't my thing. It would take a lot of work and time to rectify, let alone the inevitable hair damage. So I turned it down. Maybe this was a bad decision, I don't know, but America did have different tastes to the more with-it London at that time.

PG:
So what was happening with Mr X?

JK:
At the end of the year, just before Christmas, we went to Lincolnshire for a wonderful family time, seeing friends and going for walks on the bleak sands. He was a persistent suitor and before I knew it I was being proposed to. We did indeed get married. It happened fast. It was a quiet affair, just before Christmas 1966, and not the fairy-tale wedding I had imagined. I said I didn't mind, but I had to fight to have my parents and best friend Juliet there. It didn't feel right that he didn't want my sisters to be invited, but, clouded by the love potion, I let it go. At one point, I had a group of bookings in Paris, so off I went. Mr X came too. We rented an apartment in rue Cambon, and that was it. We settled there, and though I would come back to London for work, I would return to Paris afterwards.

One such job in London, for example, was for *Vogue* with Barry Lategan as the photographer, and with Grace Coddington styling.[2] Grace had a French boyfriend, so we also saw each other in Paris.

Jobs with Ronald Traeger were always a treat and Marit asked me to do some lovely shoots for *Vogue*. I remember doing a *Vogue* job with Ron around the time I got married, with Marit as fashion editor, changing in her apartment on the river.[3] The shoot was for suits and coats, with an umbrella as a prop, down by the river with a beautiful male model. Suddenly, there was Mr X outside Marit's apartment building. He was jealous about me working with a young man. It seems so ridiculous now, and perhaps all the more so as the young man did not, in the end, appear in the feature. After a few words, and with Ron there, we went back to work. I can't forget his words, which were, 'Jill, that man is no good for you.' He summed up the situation very quickly, but my usual instinct wasn't intact and I struggled between the extremes of such happiness, then such destructive behaviour from Mr X. This was to last, dare I say it, for fifteen years.

PG:
Jill, did you not see the dangers?

JK:
Not so clearly at the time. I realise now that I didn't have the self-assurance in my relationships that I had in my professional role. I came alive before the camera; I felt so confident and just loved giving everything to that moment. But, looking back, I realise how naïve I was emotionally, too trusting. I wanted to make people happy. I wanted to make my husband happy; and when things went wrong, I felt responsible; I felt it was my fault.

PG:
It sounds like Mr X was extremely controlling, for whatever misguided reasons, perhaps his own insecurity. What you tell me sets me thinking about that old newspaper cutting we looked at together – the article about you getting your hair cut short, soon after your marriage, encouraged by your husband.[4] Yet I am mindful of what you told me about your reluctance even to change your particular natural blonde colouring for Richard Avedon. You said there was a back-story to this seemingly innocent account.

_____

2 'The best-dressed dress', September 15th 1968
3 'Look British in corduroy country', March 15th 1967
4 Unsourced cutting found on eBay

'Look British in corduroy country', by Ronald Traeger,
British *Vogue*, March 15th 1967

JK:

Oh yes, there was indeed. I had never seen that article until you showed it to me. Perhaps now is the time to tell the full story. I have never told it before. I had no idea that Mr X had sold that version of events for his own twisted reasons. How dare he say he encouraged me to cut my hair short – and claim credit with the words, 'Jill was very brave. But I was right.' The truth is very different. This incident has been buried deep in the 'fear and shame' box.

We were in Ireland, where Mr X was due to be involved in making a film. We were in the hotel in Galway when he was told that he wasn't going to be working on the movie after all. He came up to our room, bursting with rage. After putting up with a torrent of verbal abuse and accusations that I hadn't recorded location details correctly – i.e. name of beach, time of day, exact map reference, quality of light, etcetera – I shut myself in the bathroom to get away from this tirade. But he burst in with a pair of scissors in his hand. Firstly, lashing out with his fist, he knocked me against the white tile wall, making my nose bleed. After hitting me again, he grabbed my hair and cut some off, then carried on wildly hacking at it and cutting off a lot more. I was crying and pleading for him to stop. I couldn't defend myself. Someone, I think from the hotel staff, banged on the door, complaining of the noise. Mr X told me to clean up the mess in the bathroom and then, thank God, he stormed off. I was sitting in a heap of pain and misery.

When I realised all was quiet, I shakily stood up and took stock of the wreckage. I looked shocking, battered and bruised and cut up; blood from my nose and head was spattered on the white tiles and floor, with clumps of hair scattered around. It took a long time to stop the nosebleed; then, with a towel on my pillow, I lay on the bed crying. How could this have happened? How could someone who supposedly loved me treat me in this barbaric way? My cuts, and there were several, eventually stopped bleeding. I cleaned the bathroom, lay down on the bed again and eventually fell asleep. After a week of staying in the hotel bedroom, while the swelling and bruising repaired itself, it was time to think what the hell to do next. I called a friend – Roger, from Vidal Sassoon – and asked if he would fly over to give me the best possible haircut, saying that I had tried to cut my own hair but had made a mess of it. He came to my rescue. The newspaper story was accurate in this one detail. I then told Mr X that I needed to get back home. The man was insane. Of course he begged for forgiveness and assured me he loved me. But how was I to make sense of these wild extremes?

PG:
What a wretched saga.

JK:
After every storm the sun comes out. I went home and was soon walking up in the Lincolnshire Wolds and woods, and down on the vast expanse of rippling sands. Evenings were quiet, with candlelight and log fires. I felt replenished with home-cooked food and the love of my family. I received a request from Italian *Vogue*, to do a shoot with Oliviero Toscani. I would be flown to Milan. After waking up each morning to the shock of no hair, I began to inhabit this new look with a degree of enthusiasm. I realised I was refreshed and it suited me. Vidal himself did a great job, refining the cut, and I now owned this look; so I got on the plane to go to work with confidence. Toscani was young, handsome, and friendly, with black-olive eyes that glistened; he was a good-hearted family man. The shoot, in his studio, was relaxed and simple – portrait style, sitting on a stool, just being myself – and was planned as a four-page spread. We had two days to achieve this, so we worked hard and then had a late lunch in a nearby trattoria. This was a good way to get to know the fashion editor, assistants, make-up artist, and of course Toscani. The pictures were perfect, with great classic lighting. I worked many times with him after this, on both studio and street pictures, always for *Vogue*.

PG:
I guess your work kept you going.

JK:
Yes, my work was my salvation through difficult times. It was so stimulating to be working with such great talents as Helmut, Guy Bourdin, and the young ones like Marc Hispard, but those were very challenging times. In February 1968, I had devastating news. I had recently received a rare letter, possibly the only letter, from my father. It struck me as strange because he was reminiscing about his children's beautiful childhood, how much he loved us all, how much he loved me, that he was so sorry about his illness and hoped that I was happy, and how he understood about the importance of my work. The devastating news was a phone call, which Mr X took, from the family solicitor and great friend, saying that my father had committed suicide. I was shattered; it was as if my world had collapsed, there was a massive hole beneath my feet and I needed to go home. Once there, details of what had happened were aired. Very early in the morning, Daddy had said he was going to make a cup of tea but instead he walked to an outhouse and hanged himself. Poor brother Johnty went in to the kitchen only to see my father being brought in

by Bill, the farm manager, who was in great shock. I can't imagine the scar this left on my brother, who was still so young. That week was all about caring for my mother, who was unspeakably grief-stricken and also supporting my sisters and brother. It was traumatic.

I felt bad having to return to Paris. By then I was installed in the Latin Quarter, in a gorgeous atelier. I was living there when the '68 riots were happening, the nearest I have been to a war zone. I had to be strategic about how to get home after work. The *Elle* magazine team were wonderfully helpful about ensuring that we stopped a shoot in time to get home before the chaos that usually erupted after dark. In the morning, it was awesome to see the debris of the night before: trees ripped up by their roots, cars smashed, and barricades made of piles of cobbles, prised up from the streets. These cobbles also provided plenty of ammunition to hurl at the very scary riot police. There was no mercy should a young student slip and get caught, or become penned in by mistake in a one-way street. I knew arms and legs would be broken, heads smashed, and God forbid that anyone was rounded up and put into a police van, only to emerge later in quite a bad way. The stench of tear gas was suffocating; you couldn't breathe. Only once did I get it wrong. I was walking down a side street when it became the corral. The situation got very frightening, but fortunately I was able to dive into a courtyard as the throng, followed by police with shields and batons, roared past. My heart pounding, I made it home.

PG:
So back in Paris, after your father's tragic death, how did things progress with Mr X?

JK:
Most of the time, living in Paris was a wonderful experience. Work was fun, life was fun, especially in the cool Latin Quarter, and I had friends. New friends only saw this happy side; they saw me as a stylish but laid-back, breezy beauty. And life was good in so many ways. It was possible to turn up at the busy Brasserie Lipp, for example, and a good table would be whisked up; at the best discotheques, I could waft in though there was a queue. Sundays were divine, going to the Marché aux puces, having a 3.00pm lunch, going to a movie, making love. My French was becoming natural and I would translate for Mr X. For some reason, distressingly so, his work wasn't happening. He often lost his rag over small things, which, in a kind way, I put down to his frustration. But one time, in a fit of anger, he did a deeply horrible thing – he tore into tiny shreds the precious letter from my father. He was insanely jealous of my closeness with my English friends

and family, my sisters, my mother. He was manipulative about my bookings; I put that down to his jealousy over my commitment to my work. Occasionally, he ripped up a favourite garment, wanting to hurt me. The scariest thing, though, was the odd burst of physical abuse. Over the years, there were too many incidents. I left him several times, only to find him at the airport, full of remorse, which was later followed by passionate love-making. I can't describe, or won't describe, all of it, but a weird thing would happen. I would become engulfed by a sense of shame that someone who loved me could do this to me, a sense that I was the one who should feel guilty, that for some dysfunctional reason I deserved it. I never talked to anyone about this, except when I ended up in hospital – once with a broken hand, once a broken jaw, over a foolish 'yogurt-in-glass-pots' argument. I told the medics the truth, but blamed myself. At that time, I was simply told that nobody could help me, as it was a domestic matter.

I became a master of disguising my feelings and if Mr X showed the sinister side of his Jekyll and Hyde split personality, I was able to leave the trauma at the door and go out and do a great job. I had a lovely advertising shoot for Jaeger, with Ruth Lynam, who smoked pink Sobranie cigarettes, which were so fashionable at that time. She was an experienced fashion editor and I had worked with her previously for *Life*. We went to Galway, staying in a tiny pub in Glencolumbkille on the west coast of Ireland. It was an enjoyable job and the last with my English agent, David Puttnam. After that, I worked in France, or in Italy, or would go on a trip to New York.

I often took to sitting with a coffee in Saint-Germain, reading Proust and watching the world go by. Sometimes, if I was on my own and not working, I would buy a *baguette jambon* with *cornichons* – how delicious! – and go to the Île Saint-Louis, perching on the steps by the Seine. There were many young and hungry students and artists, clearly penniless; I would often be asked to share my *baguette*, which I willingly did. Somehow, to see young people with their hardships put my story in perspective, or so I thought. I would minimise the reality of the situation, now called denial. It was very hard to deal with. But I had been born with a happy spirit, which, along with the enormous motivation that I felt for my photographic work, always won through.

I worked a lot with *Marie Claire*; the editor, 'Lala' Lazarus, had previously worked for *Jardin des Modes*. Around the time, when Dior was doing white-mask make-up, I did a beauty shoot for the magazine. Serge Lutens was the make-up man. This guy was so clever. I sat still, patient, being made up with layer upon layer of white, so that my skin colour didn't show through. After this, he applied very dramatic black eyes and then deep, really deep, red lips. It was an amazing look. The session took about five hours and we hadn't even taken a picture. I couldn't talk, laugh, or eat. Finally, when we got to take the photographs, I was asked to smoke a cigarette, letting the smoke drift slowly by. A few months later, I was doing a shoot in Greece and saw that picture on the cover of a Greek magazine. It looked cool and dramatic with the Greek lettering. So I guess it got widely published. But these glamorous images were only a part of the story. My life around this time was quite a challenge, to say the least. I needed some emotional stability, but it was hard to find. I felt so grateful to have my modelling career as a place of refuge.

La Dolce Vita

Italian magazines and photographers – discovering Rome – autographed by Federico Fellini – markets and monuments, palazzos and parties – the darker side of the city – dinner with Henry Kissinger – the eccentric Anna Piaggi – a warning from Bob Richardson – time to take stock professionally

PG:

Your work seems to have been the one area in which you could feel secure.

JK:

It gave me a focus. And now I found myself working more and more in Italy. I worked again with the charming photographer Willy Rizzo, who I had got to know a few years before on location in Beirut for a great swimwear shoot for *Marie Claire*.[1] I also started working with Italian *Harper's Bazaar*, with the art director Bob Krieger. He was so enthusiastic and I gave a lot to them over the next decade. The magazine grew through those years into a much stronger publication. But I felt there was something missing and I was all too aware of this – the real quality work that I had so enjoyed in the Sixties. I was working a lot, but too few of the jobs felt really creative. We moved to a wonderful apartment in Rome, in the Via dei Foraggi, near Foro Romano. This felt good. I worked with Oliviero Toscani once more, who was great, but my favourite among the Italian photographers was Gian Paolo Barbieri. I thought 'Thank God' when I started working with him, for Italian *Vogue* but more often French *Vogue*. I loved working with him and did so often. His studio was in Milan, where all the big magazines and advertising agencies were based. Rome was home, and Milan was work. For *Grazia* I did many trips all around Italy but also to Morocco, to Peru, and to Greenland. The magazine in those days was just like *Elle*; it was fresh. Of course, by now my Italian was pretty good, much of it learned in the food markets, which were part of a great way of life, full of warm-hearted people happy to suggest different ways of cooking.

PG:

Jill, you mention Willy Rizzo. He was quite a prominent figure in Rome's social scene and I associate him with actress Elsa Martinelli. Did you get to know them? And what was that scene like? I have a mental image of a chic, bohemian milieu – echoes of La Dolce Vita.

---

1 'dans le vent, sur la plage', June 1964

JK:

Rome was incredibly romantic. For starters, the language was seductive, while the people were open-hearted and expressive, joyous and warm. It seemed that whatever anyone did, it was done with passion. People respected others in their professions. In the small eateries, often family-run, everyone had a title, referenced with a welcoming 'Buongiorno Dottore', or 'Maestro', or for me it might simply be a friendly 'Ciao bella'. Mr X was half-Italian, but the move was more to do with work and lifestyle. After spending time there, we just decided to stay. I worked with Willy Rizzo, but he was also a lovely friend and Elsa was great. We often met up for supper before going on to something else. Elsa, always glamorous, towered over Willy; it was all great fun. One evening at Nino's, near the Spanish Steps, we were joined in the private room by Federico Fellini. He was a wonderful, large man, incredibly appealing, with a generous spirit. Elsa was so embarrassing, hassling him for an autograph between mouthfuls of risotto, flirting, and being sweet. Even as an actress and high-profile social figure, she too could be star-struck by so significant a figure. Just before we left, I asked with a smile if I could also have an autograph. I had never done this before. Federico promptly put his huge hands on my shoulders, pushed me gently round so he was behind me, slowly unzipped my dress, right down, and I wondered – with us all laughing – if I should walk away. But he then took a pen out of his pocket and with a flamboyant gesture signed his name on my back. The wall was mirrored, so I was able to watch him. 'I won't wash this off', was my first thought. This episode would be kept in my memory box.

Life was lived out and about in the city; there was so much beauty. I knew many people who lived in palazzos, both large and small, or in apartments in lovely old buildings, with views over Rome. The days buzzed, filled with lots of noise and tooting of horns in narrow, hazardous streets. Markets brimmed with colourful produce. In the evenings, you discovered another Rome, against a backdrop of softly lit ancient monuments that lifted your spirits with their beauty. Everything was delicious. Rome was a wonderful city to live in.

PG:

And Mr X?

JK:

I was mostly very happy, embracing all that life had to offer. I seemed to be in demand most of the time workwise; and we were in demand socially. The tension in my marriage was a dark storm that came about twice a year. It usually lasted two or three days, and then passed over. The intensity of the madness just disappeared, leaving intense

Le dos pudique

Les maillots à décolleté profond

Le dos-lucarne

PATRONS MARIE-CLAIRE

Le dos maillot de bain

'dans le vent, sur la plage', by Willy Rizzo, *Marie Claire*, June 1964

emotional debris. I was loved with equal intensity; and so on we went. I have a huge capacity for forgiveness, compassion, and hope. We were often stopped in the street around Via Veneto, perhaps by a chic woman cooing, '*Che bella coppia!*'. This would swell Mr X's head and his pride would expand out of all proportion.

I have never seen so many beautiful people wearing their wealth as I did in the famous Via Condotti. Caffè Greco was situated here – a great meeting place, filled with mirrors and very elegant. There were salons with tables, but you could equally just nip in for a stand-up coffee or *spremuta d'arancia*. Wonderful parties happened in Rome. The palazzos and fantastic apartments provided the backdrop to women in furs and jewellery, great looking girls in boots and skirts, stylish men, lots of green velvet jackets and cool shoes. I had a lovely ankle-length Afghan coat, which I wore a lot with a short skirt and over-the-knee boots. Some parties were very 'Dolce Vita', with too much drink and dope. Coke was coming from Hollywood. Sex was an important part of the mix, as was music. I often bumped into photographers, models, and fashion people. Veruschka and Franco Rubartelli were a hot couple, though I associate them more with Milan than Rome, as Milan was the centre of the fashion and publishing industries. They had been making remarkable pictures that turned her into a cult figure, and there was quite a buzz around their film *Stop Veruschka*, in which she appears as this extraordinary, body-painted, animal-like creature. We also had good friends who were publishers and writers.

One such couple asked us many a time to go in their lovely schooner across to some beautiful islands, and specifically a little known island called Ponza, frequented by people passing through to other islands further south. It was gorgeous, with only a couple of restaurants and markets. Huge tuna were sometimes caught in these waters, which were sparkling and clean. On one occasion in Ponza, we went with our friends on their Zodiac tender to another tiny, uninhabited island with a cove called La Cattedrale, which resembles a Gothic cathedral with its towering, sheer rocks. The turquoise water was only a few metres deep in places, carpeted with sea urchins. Gianni Lancia, the former motor manufacturer and racing enthusiast, was there on his magnificent teak yacht. We went urchin collecting: brought them up; the cook cracked them open with a knife and rinsed out the bad parts, leaving the star-shaped roe; we scooped it out with a thumb, ate it, and drank champagne – one of many great memories.

PG:
You paint a glamorous picture, though I understand there were darker undercurrents to life in Rome in the early Seventies.

JK:

Yes, there was another side to life in Rome. Bad things were unfolding in the city. There were backlashes against the rich and powerful. I heard stories of fur coats being torn off women, sometimes breaking an arm; of jewellery violently snatched from women driving with an open car window; of precious-stone rings being stolen by cutting off a woman's finger. Powerful men were kidnapped and murdered, their bodies dumped in the boot of abandoned cars. In 1973, headlines were made when John Paul Getty Jr was kidnapped for a ransom, and had an ear cut off. I thought of the happy, carefree, popular young man, often in the cafés of Piazza Navona, and the awful impact this had on him. My dentist and his wife suffered a horrendous *Clockwork Orange* ordeal, over a weekend. They survived, but were deeply scarred. Rome seemed to be a difficult place for gay guys. I knew a young actor, just starting out, who was found dead on the beach; and, in 1975, the talented film director, Pier Paolo Pasolini, who was homosexual, was murdered in never-explained circumstances on wasteland near Rome. I met Audrey Hepburn with two gorgeous gay friends, one an actor who had been in a Hitchcock film, but the consequence of such grotesque incidents and the sinister social and political undercurrents inevitably changed the mood of the city; and caution and discretion were necessary.

This was all too apparent when, one evening, I went to dinner with some friends, a family dinner with their daughter. The American statesman Henry Kissinger was there as my friend, Jojo Kingsbury-Smith, was the Hearst newspaper editor in Rome and they knew one another. Firstly, several armed bodyguards turned up and scouted the apartment as well as the guests. Next, a motorcade arrived, with Kissinger in a bullet-proof car. He was escorted in and the bodyguards took up their positions: some were outside and two were inside. We then proceeded to have a normal fun evening. The big man, who I sat next to - one of the most influential and respected political figures in the world - was totally charming.

The summers were balmy and hot. People took off for the whole of August, to country houses in Tuscany or to the coast. One of my good friends, Christina, had a wonderful farmhouse, a family gathering place where amazing cooking was a big feature. They made fresh pasta and had an outdoor oven, quite standard for farms. As well as pizza, they roasted meats in this oven. Christina and I went off foraging for salad in the fields, while her little boy ran around. We picked wild rocket and young dandelion leaves. That family gave me a true home life and were a surrogate family for years. One crazy brother had a photograph of himself in a lion's mouth, taken in Kenya. I have precious memories of those times. So although, for sure, there was a dark side to Rome, for the most part it was a seductive city where a very agreeable life could be lived among artists and creative people.

PG:
So your work kept you busy and life in Italy clearly had some very appealing aspects.

JK:
Yes, on both counts. I had no shortage of bookings and they involved interesting people and places. During my years in Rome, half my life was spent in Milan, which was the commercial centre. It worked smoothly. I would be asked to work for a magazine. The flight and hotel were taken care of and up I would go. In the winter months, Milan would be surrounded by fog and I would journey on the overnight sleeper train. I could have a gorgeous dinner, elegantly served on a white linen tablecloth, then have a peaceful night's sleep, arriving just after breakfast. It was the only reliable way to travel. I seemed to be on a cover almost every month; and once I was on six in the same season - Italian *Vogue*, Italian *Harper's Bazaar*, *Elle*, *Marie Claire*, *Linea Italiana*, and *Grazia*.

One time, I was working with Italian *Vogue* and with fashion editor Anna Piaggi. Anna, married at that time to photographer Alfa Castaldi, had an extraordinary, quite eccentric feel for fashion and dressed herself extravagantly - more so than anyone in the business. It was the time of colourful clothes, boas, and platform shoes. I remember that on one of the shoot days, in the *Vogue* studios, Bob Richardson came by to say hello. He was by now with Angelica Huston, the model and actress daughter of film director John Huston. She looked very Bob Richardson - pale and enigmatically beautiful. Bob looked sick. I had a platonic love for the fragile Bob since meeting him in New York. I felt sad that this talented and sensitive man was evidently on some other road.

It gave me a shock seeing him and reminded me of our wonderful shoots, putting me in doubt about where I was now going professionally, doing everything and anything that came my way. I was working too much, but I didn't have a supportive husband in the old-fashioned way, so when Bob said, 'You shouldn't be doing this', meaning accepting ordinary jobs rather than selecting just the extraordinary ones, I felt bruised, but I knew he was right. I was doing too many weekly magazines, which wanted my skills but sometimes left me feeling used. After a few years of this non-stop work, if I am being honest, I felt inside-out, being wanted all the time, under constant pressure but with no protection. The next time I saw Bob was a chance encounter in Saint-Tropez. I came out of the nearby fish market one day and walked slap into Bob and Norma. They were back together and they looked wrung out. We had a coffee on the port. It was wonderful to see them, but Bob was clearly not well and looking so gaunt and fragile, while Norma was doing what she could to look after him. Very sadly, that was the last time I saw him, a special talent crumbling. Bob never managed to achieve again the heights he had enjoyed at his creative peak.

PG:
So Bob's remark made you take stock?.

JK:
I was leading a full-on social life as well as being very busy with my work, and I was always being asked to parties, both in the fashion world and with friends. The fashion parties were hard to deal with. So many people seemed to want a piece of me, wanted to associate themselves with this successful English model. I had befriended an Argentinian who was a plenipotentiary affiliated to his Embassy in Rome. He was a gorgeously good-looking young man, who had such charm and managed to connect with a circle of beautiful socialites and actors. Caught up in the whirl of the Roman social scene, he seemed to be getting ever wilder. There were definitely drugs going around and eventually he went way too far and managed to destroy his life. He lost touch with reality. I suspect he was using LSD, and he was eventually dismissed. This seemed all too typical of the city at that time. I kept myself together through all of this craziness thanks to my work and to trips abroad. The big trips were so important for me, saviours of my sanity. I sighed with relief each time I set off, as I felt the pressures of Rome and a difficult relationship melt away for a while.

Travels with kindred spirits

*a first invitation from David Lean – to Kenya for Christmas –
an encounter with elephants – Peter Beard at Hog Ranch –
to French Polynesia – Christmas on the beach – a taste of paradise*

PG:
What were the most memorable trips around that time?

JK:
Surely the most exceptional trips were those I made, not for work
but purely for pleasure, to Kenya and to Polynesia with film director
David Lean and his girlfriend Sandra Hotz, known as 'Sandy', who
later became his wife. I should explain how I first met them and
how it came about. Soon after I started working in Rome, where we
stayed in a sister hotel of the Hassler at the top of the Spanish Steps,
we met up with some friends in the Via Veneto to have a drink at
Harry's Bar, and of course eat some of their delicious canapés – my
favourites being tapenade, and the tomato with anchovy and fresh
basil. Afterwards, we wandered over to the Cesarina, a lovely rustic
restaurant owned by a wonderful woman, the mama of the kitchen,
ample in size and in generosity. In the hustle and bustle of happy,
feasting people, Mr X spotted David, who he knew from London. He
rose to go and say hello and to introduce me. David told us that he
had bought a villa in the Via Appia Antica, La Mettella, 53, and would
we go for dinner the following week.

Sandy was very shy and David was a wow, a wonderful-looking man
who showed at once both strength and humility. Handsome, with
greying hair, he always wore pale blue shirts with navy jackets and
trousers; occasionally there was a white shirt but the whole time I
knew him, he never deviated from flattering navy blue. We hit it off
and our friendship became stronger over time. This must have been
around 1969-70, as he was working on *Ryan's Daughter* in Ireland,
coming and going. He used to ask me to take Sandy shopping, which
was a pleasure. Sandy had lived all her life in India and that is where
their relationship blossomed.

One day, in 1971, after *Ryan's Daughter* was wrapped up and they
were back living in Rome, David and Sandy came for supper at our
apartment, with a huge surprise announcement. They were planning
to go to Kenya and suggested we join them for a few weeks. This was
a breath-taking invitation. We went out to Nairobi for Christmas,
staying at the famous Mount Kenya Safari Club in Bill Holden's

lodge, living a dream. Rising to the sound of exotic crested birds was magical and I felt so at home in this natural environment. Every day, we went out early morning and early evening, on wildlife experiences. I tried to see Peter Beard, which didn't work out; but I was able to see David and Daphne Sheldrick. David, still the game warden of Tsavo, gave the other David lots of personal time and shared his knowledge – all heaven. We visited Daphne's elephants and had one hilarious meeting with a baby rhino and a teenage elephant, which were messing around and being generally curious.

The next leg of our journey started with pilot Jim flying us to Samburu, further north, in his twin-engine Cessna. His route took us low over the plains, heading for rivers and forests, over baobabs and alkaline water coloured pink with flamingos – a truly wonderful sight. He landed on a grass strip in an open clearing, making sure there were no animals crossing. It felt such a simple, yet exciting way to travel. Two Land Rovers were waiting for us with a small band of drivers, luggage helpers, and the obligatory tracker. These guys had eyes like eagles, noticing a crushed blade of grass, or a pad mark in the dust. They just knew if a lion had passed recently, or yesterday, and could spot whatever was out there. I became very good at being able to see that an indistinct grey patch near a thorn bush was in fact a rhino, for example, as my eyes got tuned in. David's cargo was his movie camera; Sandy was crew; Mr X was assistant; and I was friend – a friend who didn't have an agenda and was able to enjoy the honesty and authenticity of what felt like a really good friendship. This was all a privilege.

We arrived at Samburu lodge late afternoon and having seen our rooms, which were in a lovely teak-structured building with balconies and terraces overlooking the wide river, we settled into the comfortable chairs for a well-earned cup of tea. It was then that I noticed Jacqueline Kennedy and her sister, Lee Radziwill, sitting next to us, looking just like us, dishevelled and dressed for the bush. I decided to say hello, as I knew Peter was a mutual friend. After a sociable interlude, they left and we got down to making our plans for the next day. It was our hope that we might, above all, get close to some elephants, animals with an incredible sense of family. I was very excited about spending three days here. We did have an exceptional experience, the best and most wonderful part being that it was unhurried. We came across a large family, maybe twenty elephants, young ones and old ones, which had gone down to the river for a bathe. Out came the cameras, tripods, and hats; now patience was essential. We were so lucky. Hours went by as we watched them, the little ones experimenting with going a bit too deep, their trunks stretched out, and being scolded by mum and aunts, before eventually going out on to the far bank and having a glorious dust bath. When finally the sun started to go down, we returned to the lodge. I was very happy. David was very happy with what he had shot. This was the way it went. I don't know what was in his head, but it felt like a reconnaissance, or the germ of some future project; or maybe it was pure pleasure. He and Sandy had been there before; now he was sharing the experience with us.

We visited the Governor's Camp, a classy, beautiful new site, with tented rooms that included a good shower room. There was special notepaper, which I remember being gold-embossed. It was wonderful, and the food was the obligatory English cuisine, of a very high standard. We went to sleep hearing hippos in the river; and the next day we saw our first leopard as well as cheetahs hunting – we were lucky enough to witness the sixty-miles-per-hour sprint.

We returned to Nairobi for two days, before heading to Tanzania and Ngorongoro. I left a note for Peter at the New Stanley Hotel, figuring that, if he was about, he would get it. On our return, there was a reply. It said, 'To Jill Kennington, the one and only, come and visit with your friends, to Hog Ranch.' This was where Peter lived, on the Karen Blixen estate, and I persuaded David that we had to do this before we left. We took up the invitation and, not far from Nairobi, we discovered how a unique man lived.

PG:
Great for you to reconnect, I imagine?

JK:
It certainly was. I was delighted. Firstly, as we drove to the Ranch, we were greeted by wart hogs. They have a hilarious character, running with tails straight up in the air, always game for a chase. We were met by Peter, looking 'bush' and wearing shorts and sandals, as always. We had tea, brought to us by the amazing Kamante. Peter had managed to keep him on. He had been Karen Blixen's faithful man, very old by now. She had written about him in *Out of Africa*. When asked by me how old he was, he replied in moons. The tent was something out of another era. I was struck by how big it was. Apart from an area with bed and mosquito net, it was like a studio-cum-writing space with a desk littered with photographs and writings, and with more pictures and papers pinned to the canvas. Peter told us he had caught a poacher and had strung him up on a tree like leopard bait – he was now in some trouble with the police. Poaching was already a catastrophic problem to solve; and now, all these years later, it seems to be even worse, still not eradicated. I could willingly have lived there. I loved it.

Peter and Africa are unforgettable, like the setting sun. The day before we left Nairobi, we were asked to have curry at the home of David and Sandy's travel agent. Invited for midday, we all assumed it was for lunch, but the cooking only started after we arrived. We must have been there for about five hours, but it was a pleasure in itself to see at first hand how the food was prepared with such respect and to enjoy engaging and timeless conversation.

Back to Rome, from where I went on to Paris for my booked work with Gian Paolo Barbieri. This was for an Yves Saint Laurent advertising shoot with French *Vogue*. I was also booked with Jacques Rouchon for an editorial job with Italian *Harper's Bazaar*. Courrèges clothes were the subject. Courrèges himself kept trying to persuade me to do the shows. There was still a huge difference between the catwalk girls, who always seemed old fashioned, and photographic models like me, who seemed to be on trend. I wasn't persuaded and politely declined.

PG:
Your time in Rome certainly was punctuated with memorable travels. Now tell me about Polynesia.

JK:
Back in Rome, it was hard to get back into my regular working and social life. I was still in love with Africa and it took me a long time to settle. I have always had a bag packed, ready for a trip. And there were lots of trips up to Milan for jobs, and it was great that I was working. But the friendship with David and Sandy was strong and true, and led to another wonderful travel opportunity. Halfway through the year, we were asked to join them for the weekend as they had a surprise. Screenplay-writer Robert Bolt was leaving on the Saturday, having been with them for a week. He always left a trail of ash around the house, as he smoked but let the ash grow like a worm until it fell where it wished. Friday was fun, then Sandy and I went with Fulvio, their man, to the fish market, to buy beautiful big prawns for a curry that night. Before dinner, the surprise popped out of David's mouth. Would we go to French Polynesia with them the next Christmas, allowing two months for the trip? I nearly fell out of my chair. What an amazing proposal.

PG:
Wow. So another great trip to look forward to?

JK:
Life went on, but yes, it certainly was wonderful to have this to look forward to. The date finally arrived, mid-December. We flew to Los

Angeles, checking in to the Beverly Hills Hotel. On the flight from London was a trendy young couple who canoodled the whole way over to L.A. It was the rock singer Rod Stewart, dressed in a turquoise velvet suit, with his glamorous girlfriend of the moment. He was performing in a club in Beverly Hills, which we were invited to. He was great. Then on we went to Tahiti, first class, flying in over black volcanic beaches before we landed. We went to the hotel to be met by David and Sandy. Garlands round my neck, the smell of frangipani, and a pineapple punch – it was the start of an exotic trip around the islands, Moorea, Huahine, and Raiatea, heading for Bora Bora.

All these islands were magical. We flew over white beaches, a steaming mountain and forests in a little prop plane, coming in to land on small grass airstrips. We stayed one night on each, but we would have a longer spell in Bora Bora. Next we took off in a small seaplane, over a deep blue ocean. As we neared Bora Bora, the water turned to strong emerald green, then, as we came in to land, inside the big reef that surrounded this island, it turned a vivid turquoise, with bright white sand. We wooshed in and stopped at the over-water quay, where we were met in a Boston whaler that took us to the only hotel.

Bora Bora was a dream world. The small hotel consisted of the main hut, reception, boutique, bar, circular dining room with a staggering outlook across the big lagoon to the reef, open window frames with no glass but shutters that could be battened down when stormy. We had a fruit punch at the outside bar before going to our rooms. Every evening, this bar was alive with locals. Pretty boys who had been brought up as girls, which is what Tahitians did if they wanted a daughter, and guests happily mingled to the sounds of Tahitian music. It was a wonderful, joyous, colourful place. Bungalows were dotted about the gardens, under the palm trees, but we had two of five exquisite ones sited over the water. The bed was strewn with fresh flowers and the deck overlooked the lagoon, with steps down to the water. This was the most beautiful place I had ever been.

Night-times were an awesome experience. Having come back from dinner, as we sat on the deck in silence, suddenly, and clearly visible in the light under the deck, there appeared the ghostly shape of a giant manta ray. It swept up from the darkness, opening its mandibles like welcoming arms, to guide plankton straight into its huge gaping mouth; then in, up, and on to its back, showing its white underbelly and gills, looping the loop. Mesmerised, I watched for about half an hour as it repeated this ritual, before gliding off into the dark. Every night, the visitor came, knowing the plankton would be there, attracted by the light.

Day one, and we were going out on a Boston whaler, with a cool-box full of drinks and fruit. Alex, the manager, was a very funny young man, more than willing to give David his help and advice. There was also a local guy who knew every reef and lagoon. Before we went, we had a meeting with the underwater expert, who gave tips on what fish we would encounter and what to do, should we meet a shark. He said the sharks shouldn't worry us as they had plenty of reef fish to eat here, but to keep our eye on them and, if concerned, swim slowly back to the boat. Okay! The place we stopped at was a lagoon within a lagoon, once again a staggering colour. Once moored, David did some filming of Sandy looking regal, then of me, waist-deep in the water and then walking out. I felt nibbles at my feet, from several baby sharks that had been born in the still shallows. On our return, David had a message from the film producer Dino de Laurentis, who was pestering him for a meeting, which David was trying to avoid. We were there for Christmas, but blow me down if De Laurentis didn't send out his son to try and befriend David. I sent a telegram to Eileen Ford, thinking that I would love to go to New York on the way back.

Days were spent on the reef, looking for tiger cowries and, every day, I snorkelled in the crystal-clear waters, meeting parrot fish, trumpet fish, and many other species, with enough time to really mingle and observe them. Some were really amusing. One day, a family of giant manta rays were messing about quite close to the hotel. Checking first, I took off to swim with them. They reminded me of slow-motion butterflies because of their triangular shape, spanning fifteen feet across. They played so gracefully, swimming in spirals, with scrolling tails at the back and mandibles, often in a corkscrew shape, at the front. I couldn't quite believe what I was doing here. I also managed to give them a couple of strokes. Later, over supper of mahi-mahi, the local dolphinfish, I tried to recall the emotional experience. David was looking great and content; Sandy was looking beautiful and smiley; and Mr X was good as gold, as David was the only man I ever felt he respected. Life was sweet.

Christmas was amazing. We all joined in a French-Polynesian feast on the beach, to be served at sundown. It took all day to prepare. All hotel guests were on one very long table, strewn with coconuts, exotic fruit, and flowers laid down the middle on hand-plaited palm fronds. There were spit-roasted piglets and chickens, basted with sweet- and sour-tasting marinades and, of course, a huge mahi-mahi, decorated with cucumber. Suddenly, an outrigger appeared with Father Christmas on board, dressed the western way in red, and sporting a white beard. He had a huge sack with little presents for all the local children, who jumped around in excitement. The dancing women with their grass skirts, and the dancing men wearing green leaf headdresses and loin cloths, accompanied by a group of musicians, made for a truly wonderful scene for a Christmas Day. The chef was drinking too much rum, so Alex, the manager, felt highly stressed. He later told us that it wasn't the first time that this Chinese chef had got drunk, retiring to his hut apparently to watch porn films. He would have to go. After the next two weeks, spent getting to know every beach, bay, and lagoon, it was time to leave. We had enjoyed great conversations about all sorts of subjects, lots of movie stories, and lots of laughs. David was cooking an idea. So, back to Rome, back to work. I felt sated with sun and health and contentment.

Jill, by Gian Paolo Barbieri, French *Vogue*, June-July 1974

From Sudan to Greenland

a creative rapport with Gian Paolo Barbieri –
to the Sudan for French Vogue *–*
to Peru, then Greenland for Grazia

PG:
Jill, so back in Rome and back to work?

JK:
I should tell you more about one Italian photographer I really enjoyed working with, Gian Paolo Barbieri. I believe that, as I matured, this professional liaison was exactly what I needed. He totally understood women, beauty, glamour, and his lighting was superb, quite theatrical, with something of the flavour of old Hollywood movies. He always used this wonderful creative make-up artist, who just had an instinct for star quality work and created beautiful hairstyles. They might be straight, or might be tightly curled and then undone with her hands, no brushes, to look just so alive – her work had really strong allure. The look would often be further dramatised by the studio wind machine. I could completely work the feeling and atmosphere. The clothes were classy. Barbieri worked a bit like Avedon, creating a real excitement in the studio, and he had a wonderful sense of style. I vividly remember one time when we shot glamorous evening clothes in a studio in Rome that made me feel like a movie star.

French *Vogue* was a gorgeous magazine to work for, and so in tune with Barbieri. We were asked by Francine Crescent, the terrific editor, to go to Sudan – a very exciting prospect. The shoot became the cover and lead story for a great summer issue.[1] I believe the trip was sponsored for *Vogue* by the super-wealthy Adnan Khashoggi, in return for which the magazine was to give his wife a few pages as she was trying to make her mark as a reportage photographer.

We had a great adventure, shared with a brilliant writer called Simone Brousse. Our little team made photographs in Khartoum, at the palace so full of history and its association with Gordon of Khartoum. The President gave us the use of his romantic private riverboat. I had an adorable chimpanzee as my friend on board. Then we made our way to the docks. I remember Barbieri saying in his strong Italian accent, 'I want a camel suspended in the air.' And indeed, his wish

---

1 'Soudan pays de l'éternel', June–July 1974

was fulfilled. It was a mad idea and was pulled together a bit like a John Cowan shoot from a decade before. Yours truly, the ever-intrepid self, was winched on to the roof of a building; then the poor camel, strapped into a harness, was lifted high up in the air, legs dangling – not something we would do today. The picture was wildly eccentric, with cargo ships as a backdrop. Next, we made a trip to the pyramids in the desert and a stunning camel was produced for me to ride. We had a long journey to the medieval Red Sea port of Suakin, a magic place built in pale stone that gave an impression of having been bleached by the sun and the reflected light off the salt water. Here we did a photograph with a dugong, a sort of freshwater hippo; and another with a small shark on my head.

Then we headed up to Port Sudan where arrangements were made to take us out to a coral reef, to shoot swimsuits underwater. I had never seen such crystal-clear water. The reef was amazing, full of colour, next to a precipice that fell away deeply into the void. We then flew down to Juba, our last location, on Khashoggi's private plane. This is where we made some photographs that remain favourites – one with me languishing in a hammock and another with, of all things, a small crocodile. I was wearing it like you would a stole. It had been given some tranquillisers, and its snout was tied tightly just in case it became troublesome. I waded out into the river and stood there with this prehistoric creature around my shoulders, hoping for the best. I also loved this shoot as I had a natural look, using minimal, improvised make-up that I had bought in a Sudan market as Mr X had stomped on my own in a wild rage before I left Rome. Once again, as you can imagine, I was relieved and excited to get away and enjoy my role on such an exotic trip.

I remember so well the heat and dust of the market and surrounding streets, in Port Sudan, in Khartoum, and in the deserted little port of Suakin. But my most vivid impressions were of the diverse peoples, drawn from many different tribes, and with striking differences. The Ethiopians were the most beautiful. They had such elegance. Their lithe and lean bodies, which had evolved in response to a hard way of life, had a natural grace – a lesson for westerners. Many wore tight corn rows, tiny close-to-the-head plaits. Of course these were practical, but the style also showed off so well the wonderful shape of their heads. Women dressed in colourful sarongs and had material wrapped around their heads – such panache. I returned to Rome knowing that we had created a strong feature and wondering where the next trip might take me.

'Soudan, pays de l'éternel', by Gian Paolo Barbieri,
French *Vogue*, June-July 1974

PG:
Your jobs provided you with remarkable opportunities to see the world.

JK:
They most certainly did. And the Rome years, through the Seventies, provided just as many opportunities as I had enjoyed in the Sixties, when I was based in London. I went on a lovely trip with *Grazia* to Peru with photographer Giovanni Lunardi. We zig-zagged far up into the mountains by train to the magical Machu Picchu. Staying up there in a small lodge was a wonderfully peaceful experience. The other amazing trip for *Grazia* was to Greenland, with photographer Franco Petazzi. He, like Lunardi, was a regular *Grazia* contributor at this time. I could hardly believe that I was going to the Arctic for the second time in my life. This was very different from my last experience. The small Inuit settlement that was to be our base took some getting to. We spent the first night in the international airport, where there was an American air base. We then hopped from village to village, up the western coast, in a helicopter piled with supplies. En route, doctors were dropped off and post and food supplies were delivered until we eventually landed in Jakobshavn. The reason this particular location was chosen was that it was known as the place where icebergs originated. They would break off and drift out of the fjord, majestic, gently gliding mountains of ice - a wondrous sight. The bay was generally calm, so the reflections in the mirror-like water were truly awe-inspiring. We stayed in the small wooden hotel that had been built for the Danish shrimp-fishing people who came over to manage this business. It was as warm as toast. One lasting memory I cherish is of enjoying hot, steaming shrimps for breakfast. They were served in a huge barrel and we helped ourselves.

When it became dark, which it did very early, we photographed in the village. We went to the little local school and the beautiful round-faced children clamoured about, looking at my clothes and face and make-up. We made pictures on a fishing boat, full of harpoons. Every so often, the local hunters would catch a whale and the giant creature was landed in the harbour to be cut up for food. It seemed a tragic sight, but for the local people it meant survival. The very best of experiences was our last day of shooting, with two guides and two sleds, each with a team of huskies. Setting off from the village we had a bumpy ride, hard work for the huskies, but then we arrived at a bay and, having tested the ice, we slid on to it. Woosh - we were gliding along on this endless flat surface, going at a great pace, with the guide running and shouting his team on. The shushing sound of sled on ice together with the sight of these tremendously strong huskies running at a hell of a lick, tails curled up - sometimes changing places from outside to inside on their long harnesses – was an unforgettable sensation. When we had shot the last of our photographs, the art director Massimo Cianieri took off by himself and to my surprise I saw him light a small bonfire on which he was clearly burning something. Gold flames shot up from white ice. He later told me he was burning the love letters he had written to me, but had never dared give to me.

The huskies lived outside. They were often restless and howled to each other. They were so tough, sleeping out in temperatures as low as 40 degrees below zero. They would curl up in a tight ball, noses to the base of their tails, to preserve their body heat. Once, in daylight, I saw a child hauling a frozen curled-up huskie that had died in the night, pulling it like a sled. Only the fit survived this harsh life. This trip had been another privilege to be enjoyed; and when our little team left, we had a lovely send-off, with smiling Inuit faces and waves from the people we had encountered or who had helped us. My next stop would be French Polynesia, to enjoy a second trip – this time also a two-month stay – with David Lean and Sandy. I recall leaving Greenland, where it was 35 degrees below zero and arriving in Tahiti, where it was a balmy 30 degrees above – from fur coats and big boots to a sarong and bare feet.

From fur coats to a sarong

*back to Kenya with David Lean – Lake Turkana – beautiful people,
extraordinary landscapes – a second trip to French Polynesia –
Gauguin women – undefined expectations –
home via Los Angeles – Fred Astaire*

PG:
*Jill, you have shown me your passport from those years. The stamps give a
hint of the extent of your travels. So you had a second trip to Polynesia?*

JK:
Yes, I seized every opportunity I could to experience different
cultures and scenery. And yes, we went back to Polynesia with David
and Sandy. But before that, in 1974 and prior to the Greenland trip,
we had made a second trip to Kenya with them. I should tell you
about that first. This time, our first stop was Kilimanjaro. Driving
to a farmstead through now-neglected fields given over to Africans,
one could only imagine how beautiful and well-managed they had
once been. It would probably take years to get them looking healthy
again. There was a lot of misguided government reclamation from
the white farmers, leaving shattered families. The house that was
our destination, nestling in the foothills and close to the forest edge,
was rambling and very comfortable, with huge log fires; but the most
amazing aspect was looking through the windows at the view – one
could only gasp at the glory of this huge flat-topped mountain.

Flying up to Lake Rudolf – now called Lake Turkana after the tribe
of semi-nomadic people native to this territory – was like flying
over the moon, for below us stretched a vast area of inhospitable
terrain, craggy and dusty. It was hard to imagine how the people
could survive. Meagre patches of grass and thorn trees were the diet
of their livestock – camels, goats, and zebu cattle. Water was drawn
from small wells. I could see little settlements of maybe four or five
round mud huts, shaped so that the winds swept around and over
them. Some settlements were abandoned, the people and their cattle
having moved on to find more food. Theirs was an extremely tough
existence. They were a noble, handsome people, lean and fit, gracious,
and striking for their distinctive and vivid bead collars, headdresses,
and body adornments.

This place had a savage magic. The camp had a couple of very good
modern fishing boats, for rich clients who came up here to fish for

the huge Nile perch – enormous but placid. We were taken out to visit an uninhabitable island, full of sea birds, including my favourite – pelicans. David did a lot of filming again, stacking up reels of personal footage, apparently all housed now by the British Film Institute. Somewhere in that archive is footage of me running down the huge, rolling sand dunes. This was a landscape that made an indelible impression. I can never forget its scale and character. Peter Beard had come up here to shoot for his book on crocodiles, *Eyelids of Morning: The Mingled Destinies of Crocodiles and Men*.[1] We saw many crocs. The bays of the lake were alkaline, with slimy and frothy jade-green edges; the crocodiles lived in the fresh water that came down from the Nile, through the border with the Sudan. They slithered silently or just lurked ominously, waiting for as long as it took to snap a meal.

We spent about three days in the Serengeti. From here we went back to Nairobi and then returned to Rome and work. Trips such as this were inspiring, but also strangely unsettling. They made me feel I wanted to live a different life. These journeys were just so enriching and gave me great perspectives on the world and my place in it. Fashion and beauty seemed insignificant and frivolous in comparison with these confrontations with nature on an epic scale.

PG:
I can appreciate your conflicted emotions, the effect of these experiences and how they put the pattern of life in Rome, and of your work as a model, into a different perspective. But before you tell me about the challenges that awaited you in Rome, do tell me about that second trip to Polynesia.

JK:
My second and last visit to French Polynesia came directly after the wonderful working trip to Greenland in 1975. The contrast was extreme. I got myself, via Paris and Los Angeles, on to a plane to Tahiti, first-class luxury and very spoiling. Then, having thrown off the warm clothes for simple garb, I headed for our reunion in Bora Bora. It was incredible to be back. And wonderful to see the Gauguin women once again, with their incredibly long hair, often reaching down to the backs of their knees. Coconut oil was used for both skin and hair.

A Frenchman, Serge, rugged, with tousled hair, was to be our guide. He gave me the best smile, one of friendliness. He proved himself a capable man. That evening, at the over-water bar, we talked about

---

1 1973

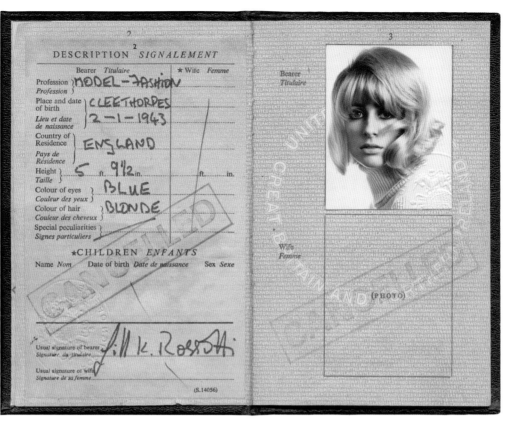

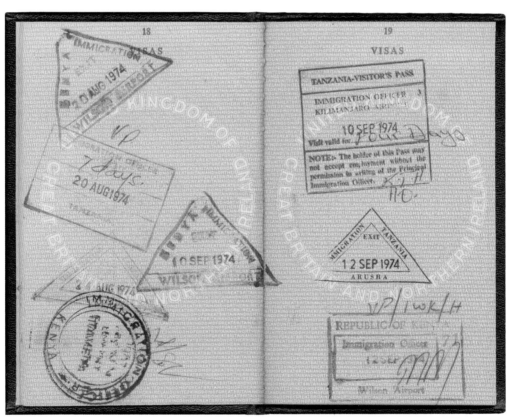

Jill's passport

plans for the next day. With him was Martine, a very young Tahitian girl, compact and sexily curvaceous, with a mop of coconut-oiled hair and a giggly, smiling personality. Straight away, on introduction, she gave us all two kisses.

The plan was to go out by small plane to one of the largest atolls in the world, Rangiroa. David was really excited about this, as he said it would be very wild. We set off, and as we approached our destination I could see the atoll, surrounded by its substantial dark ring of coral reef, with bright turquoise-blue water inside the lagoon. It was huge; the other end wasn't even visible while the other side was at quite a distance.

Serge took us through the turquoise lagoon where we beached for our picnic stop, under some messy palms. First, he and Martine collected dead coral and lit a fire. Then Serge took me and Martine quite a way out to sea, where she could fish with her harpoon. She would dive down and come straight up again with the harpooned fish held high out of the water, to avoid shark interest, and drop it in the boat. She caught seven fish and I was shocked to see her eat one right there in the boat. It was still alive and her white teeth just gnashed into the fillets, ripping them off. She just laughed at my reaction. From then on, I called her 'cannibal', with the French pronunciation.

I gazed into the clear water of the reef pools, which revealed deep purple sea urchins, a wondrous sight. The colour reminded me of my first Mini. I was able to collect some strewn spines and Martine made me a necklace, boring small holes at the inner end and tying each one on to plaited coconut fibre – so pretty. That afternoon, we went by boat to another part of the reef that had lagoons within lagoons, and still smaller lagoons within. We came across a man studying a beached sixteen-foot tiger shark, which was fascinating to look at.

It was all so wild and untouched by humanity, just nature, somehow very humbling. This was a valuable experience. David was windblown and happy; Sandy was like a sister and I was so happy. I did the half-mile walk over to the other side of the reef. It was windy here and the ocean looked so deep and mysterious. It was a place for reflection. I couldn't help thinking that David had plans; he had filmed a lot this time, plenty of footage of me and footage of Sandy, often at the over-water bar, looking off into the distance and straight at the camera – was he preparing for something, I wondered? I revelled in my amazing adventures. But I was also increasingly sensitive to an unspoken dimension to David's interest in me. I was starting to feel that perhaps the relationship with him wasn't quite right. While the situation between us all had at first seemed so carefree, I now felt under a certain pressure and was uncomfortable at having to live up to expectations that I couldn't quite define, or expect to fulfil. Nothing was said, but I had a sixth sense that this would be my last such trip with David and Sandy.

Soon, it was time to leave this extraordinary environment and head back home to reality. David and Sandy flew on to New Zealand to catch the QE2 and travel home in luxury. We flew to Los Angeles, where we spent a few days. Phil Kellogg, David's agent, took us out for dinner in Rodeo Drive and introduced me to Fred Astaire, who was having a quiet supper. He was twinkly and so appealing. Then back to Rome. Once again, it was hard to settle back into normal life.

Interlude in Saint-Tropez

*professional anxieties - constant tensions -
to Saint-Tropez to work with Helmut Newton - the delights of Saint-
Tropez - a growing sense of powerlessness*

PG:
*Jill, you make no reference to Mr X on these trips. What is going on in your
relationship? How do things unfold back in Rome after these remarkable
travels?*

JK:
Well, for one thing, work after that last trip to Polynesia was less
appealing. At that stage in my life, I found myself dying to be me. I
felt that with some work, for the smaller magazines rather than the
high fashion and glossy shoots, I wasn't really doing myself justice. It
was, of course, always reassuring to be offered jobs, but I wasn't being
selective. I felt as if I was being drained of my independence, used,
and my creativity eroded. Meanwhile, our lease on the Rome flat was
coming to an end, so I was looking for something else. Through a
friend who was an advocate, I saw an amazing jewel of an apartment
in Via Condotti, with a roof garden. It was close by the wonderful
Caffè Greco. The lease would involve a commitment of many years. I
fell in love with it. It was a perfect size and not too big. Mr X wouldn't
commit and I remember being devastated. The view was wonderful
- Rome's rooftops; look up the street and you saw the Spanish Steps,
down the street the Hassler Hotel. I wanted to curl up in this great
apartment and refuse to leave. David gave us the use of his home
on the Via Appia Antica, so we had space and time for decisions.
Unfortunately, Mr X was constantly criticising the housekeepers,
Margarita and Fulvio, to such an extent that they contacted David
to report how, when I was away working, he would lord it over them.
How embarrassing and disrespectful, especially as this hospitality
was so kind of David and Sandy.

A break came when I was offered a job in Saint-Tropez, with Helmut.
We stayed, as usual, at the Ferme d'Augustin, near Pampelonne, above
Club 55, then just a tiny beach eatery. Well, I just stayed on. Mr X
insisted on coming over for a few days' break before the job finished.
Mr X was constantly telling me that at my age I shouldn't still be
working. How wrong he was; but I hate arguments. Suddenly I was
confronted with the fact that this had to be the moment to make a
new start. I spent many hours just walking, feeling the sea breezes,
smelling the warm pine trees, feeling my way, trying to find the right

decision. After about a month, I contacted a friend, Pierre, an estate agent I had met years before with Helmut. He arranged for us to rent an apartment he had bought for his wife, Nellie. It was lovely, above the Restaurant La Ponche, overlooking the Place des Ramparts by the harbour. It was in a large house, with the Minister of Culture living above and the celebrated French artist Bernard Buffet below. There were also two sitting tenants, an old man and a hippie with dreadlocks who was a musician.

PG:
So you moved in?

JK:
Yes, it was irresistible. Saint-Tropez was a wonderful mixture. The sun was always out, and in the early morning the boulangeries and patisseries were hard at work, the breads and *croissants* with their sweet aromas giving way later in the morning to pastries and cakes. I would buy a *baguette*, sometimes bumping into people who hadn't been to bed yet and were in need of a *pain au chocolat*. Then I would go to the vegetable and fruit stalls near the fish market. I loved chatting to the stallholders, many of whom were already drinking their pastis. Madeleine, who owned a fish stall, was a fabulous woman, and gave me so many tips on how to cook certain things, for example *écrevisses à la neige*. This was a truly delicate soup of freshwater crayfish, so light. But you have to buy the crayfish alive. There is a way of holding the middle section of the tail, twisting and pulling the tract out – horrible to do – then dropping the poor little things into the boiling water.

We often met up with people at Sénéquier, the main café on the harbour front, with its red canvas seats and awnings. It was an amazing people-watching and bumping-into-people place and plans were made there for the evening. Saint-Tropez was full of wannabe-spotted visitors; a lot of posing went on. The big boats were moored opposite, the gin-palace type with ostentatious bouquets of orange gladioli on the table. Often a browned-to-a-crisp, elderly and obviously rich man, wearing a tropical suit, would appear with – guess who – a delicious young beauty. The reverse also happened – a bejewelled elderly woman, bronzed and lined, would have a pretty boy or two at her beck and call. Gay couples, high on being where it's at, showed off, kissing and clasping each other as they slid along the quay. Very handsome young men and expensive young women were happy to play the hippie in Saint-Tropez on Saturdays, which was market day, in the Place des Lices, crowding out the old men who usually played *boules*. One might catch sight of Brigitte Bardot, who would drive over in her Mini-Moke, the back packed with her dogs, to do some shopping.

Many days were spent on private boats. A friend, married to a crazy English girl, had, as he liked to boast, the fastest boat in the Mediterranean. It looked like a grey naval vessel, yet was luxurious inside. He had a cool skipper but, unlike other boats, no other crew. We would go with him to the islands, or down the coast, the skipper cooking lunch of roasted porcini and pasta. After about six weeks, I began to realise that this was not for me. I was eating beautiful food, enjoying the pleasures of hanging out at Club 55, chatting over an artichoke, or a spider crab, going to parties in luxurious villas and nightclubs, or giggling around my friend Annie's pool with a salad at 3.00pm. But I needed to work. I needed a focus. I thought I would go mad if I carried on living this life in the South of France, which did not give me the space I needed from an increasingly critical and coercive husband. Sometimes, I could tell by his whisky drinking that he was gearing up for a black mood. I could smell it, a pungent acid smell that frightened me; then he would blow a gasket and be horrible and destructive. The next day would be a display of 'Please forgive me. It won't happen again. You know I worship you and love you and need you.' Anyway, I suggested that I could and would love to design clothes. I would need to learn properly. I could go to Rome and stay with our American friends in the palazzo in Trastevere. It was agreed that I would go and do some research. I had a lucky and productive visit. Lancetti, a very good and gentle designer, said that I could be an apprentice for as long as I wanted, four days a week. This was all perfect and I could stay with my friends. I was due to begin this new chapter in November, just two months away.

I was really excited about this plan and, back in Saint-Tropez, I thoroughly enjoyed the next few autumn weeks, getting to know more locals. The village became its own again after the summer crowds had gone and I got to know every nook and cranny. There were a couple of bad scenes when I got locked out by Mr X. The old man upstairs asked me in, to get warm. He was very kind; he kept saying that Mr X was an alcoholic and that he would only get worse. As we got to within three weeks of my Rome trip, there was a terrible outburst of anger because I came back from the market with the wrong fish. He was being totally inflexible and controlling all the time. He manipulated this confrontation, using it to put pressure on me to pull the plug on the Rome plan. I realised how powerless I was and felt deeply miserable. About a month after this outburst, with the Rome plans now cancelled, he suddenly suggested - quite out of the blue - that I might like to go away for a few months and visit my favourite uncle in New Zealand.

New Zealand

*family and friends on the other side of the world – a blunt question –
time spent in the landscape, from deserted beach to volcano crater –
a telegram – issues to be confronted*

PG:
So you went to the other side of the world?

JK:
I could hardly believe that the day had actually arrived. I was fully
expecting the same pattern as before and that Mr X would go into a
black mood at the last minute. However, he took me to the airport in
our little Ferrari, which came out of the garage for a spin, and I was
off to New Zealand without a hitch. My visa was for six months and
we agreed that I could stay that long. The flight out was unbelievably
wonderful. I was so happy that I had this trip to myself, to visit cousins
who I hadn't seen since they were very young children, my favourite
uncle, Gordon, and his wife Celia, with the prospect also of precious
time to myself. A family gang picked me up from the airport and
drove me to their farm, stopping for a frozen yogurt on the way. I felt
hugely welcomed with screams of joy from Celia and plenty of hugs.

On day one, Gordon asked me to take Bess, their beautiful Clydesdale,
around the farm, up and down the tracks, to get to know the lay of
the land. I rode bareback on this gentle giant, feeling the wind in my
hair, cobwebs blowing away. We rode past the lazy dairy herd, heads
down munching, past the ponds, where later my sixteen-year-old
cousin showed me how to roll a canoe, then past the woods inhabited
by glow-worms, and then the wetlands, down past the crops of soya
beans. It was glorious. When it was time for supper, Gordon told me
I would have to earn my keep, which meant I would be helping with
the milking at 4.30am. Also, there was a field of ragwort that needed
pulling – roots up, ragwort killer in the hole, then on to the next one. I
will never forget this huge field covered in the yellow plants that were
so poisonous to livestock. My young cousin, Paul, who was sixteen at
the time, gradually succeeded in clearing the field during the week.
Gordon made a plan to go climbing and camping for a few days with
me and my cousin Lynn, who was ten years younger than me.

In order to assess my fitness, Gordon took me to an amazing gorge. We
went down, crossed the bed and climbed up the other side to the top
ridge. I could see for miles and found myself striding along the edge
quite happily on my own. Then Gordon called out, his voice echoing

round the gorge walls, and gesticulated that I was to come back to him. We sat down to take in the magnificence of the landscape. He turned to me and said that I had looked like a Masai warrior, thin and strong. What he said next, though, came as a shock. 'Now Jill, what is going on with your marriage?' Suddenly, I was drawn back to my difficult circumstances, which I never talked about. Unbeknown to me, my mother had written to my uncle saying she was so happy that I was visiting and would he talk to me about my situation. I totally spilled over, telling him that I was unable to keep Mr X happy, that I always seemed to make him angry, and that it was all my fault. He told me in his wise way that this was rubbish, that I was wonderful and must believe in myself, must trust my instincts, must remain true to my inner being. I needed to be reassured of these things and it was very humbling to hear him being so unwaveringly supportive, full of good sense and affection. He told me that I was like a flower beginning to bloom. New Zealand and family were good for me. This was what I had been missing, as, when I was with Mr X, he had manipulated and isolated me from my old friends and my family.

Week two, and I took a driving test, passed, and was then free to use the assortment of farm vehicles. I visited Lynn on her boysenberry farm, picking fruit for three days and sleeping on the beach with two American friends of the family. I had a beautiful time, talking under the stars and cooking on the fire we made. There was no one else on what was a five-mile stretch of white sand, edged with dunes. In this environment, I felt like an onion, shedding layers to reveal the real me, clean and free. I drove to the village, a simple settlement just like those in the Westerns – one street of wooden buildings, with verandas and a chair or two on the deck. There was a bank, a store selling food, a farm supply shop, and a clothing store, which was where I was headed. I found good socks, shorts, boots for walking, a New Zealand vest – which was a simple wool vest you wore next to your skin – and a sweater. I wore the boots straight away to start breaking them in. We were to walk up a volcanic mountain and sleep in a crater. The night before we left, I got a telegram from Mr X. I chose to ignore it, but then sent one back saying, 'Just off on a trip, all's well and happy.' We set off and arrived at the foot of the mountain, ready for our trek.

The trip was dramatic, both for the landscapes, which were breathtaking, and the weather, which had nasty surprises in store. When we reached the crater rim, after a long hike over lava fields, we went over and down into an enormous black bowl, with a turquoise lake at the bottom. It was as strange and austere as the moon. We set up camp at the bottom, but that night a huge and unexpected storm developed with swirling, roaring winds that literally whipped away our tents and left us wet, cold, and utterly miserable. We retraced our steps by torchlight and eventually found shelter in a hut, where we managed to get warm and caught a few hours of sleep. With the dawn, and clothes nearly dry, we set off again, taking a short cut back to our vehicle.

PG:
Was it now time to confront the telegram from Mr X?

JK:
When we got back to the farm, it was bathed in sunshine and full of birds chirping and singing in the early evening, which made our recent adventure seem quite unreal. On the kitchen table lay another telegram from France. I let it sit there. I walked around this lovely homely house, designed on one level with French windows in every room, past Celia's loom and her homespun wool, and out onto the veranda. This zig-zagged, so there was always a sunny side on which to sit and look out to the beautiful, undulating landscape beyond. After some quiet reflection, I went to the kitchen and picked up the latest telegram. It burned my hand. I knew it was trouble. I opened it and it said simply, 'Come back, I need you here.' Fury welled up. Here I was, for six months I thought, away from criticism, finding myself, finding peace. And after only two and a half weeks I was being asked to return. It was summer, glorious warmth. Cousin Paul took me to see the glow-worms after dark that night. This was magical. It was like looking into a doll's house, only smaller. It conjured up thoughts of magic palaces, with little lights in each room, a glimpse of the busy life of tiny creatures. The telegram burned in my pocket. I would have to deal with it. Back at the house, our supper of roast hogget and greens from the vegetable patch was interrupted by the telephone. It was Mr X telling Gordon that I had to come back. I heard Gordon say that we had plans to go to South Island for the next few weeks and that we would be in touch after that. Obviously the conversation became difficult and I was called to the phone. I could sense the control and manipulation in his voice; then after the calm came the storm. He said he had been diagnosed with cancer and he needed me to come back, that there were hospital visits and appointments. My logic told me none of this was true, but he kept up the pressure, and I weakened, and agreed to come back. I felt that I had betrayed myself. I didn't believe him, but at the same time, for some mad reason, felt dutiful. Married for life through thick and thin, for better for worse – whose words were these? I was the other side of the world, but I still felt trapped. Well, I had to deal with this problem and, reluctantly and many tears later, I was on the plane to France.

Escape

*deception and entrapment in Saint-Tropez –
a nightmare scenario – demons confronted –
escape via Nice to the love and security of family*

PG:
You were taking a very difficult initiative. What awaited you in France?

JK:
I arrived at Nice airport and got a taxi to Saint-Tropez. As I reached
the apartment, I felt a tight knot in my stomach. I opened the door
to find Mr X lying on the sofa, with a pretty girl at his feet, literally
sitting on the floor next to him. I saw her sudden look of desperation
and I immediately wanted to reassure her. I thanked her and told her
she could leave. This was the daughter of people who had a beautiful
sailing boat and had been moored for months on the quay. Mr X's
foot was bandaged. I was right to have been sceptical. He didn't have
cancer, but a severe case of gout. I felt cheated. I unpacked my things,
opened the wardrobe and there was nothing in it. It transpired that,
in a fit of rage at me not being there for him, he had ripped up all my
clothes. I was shocked and frightened. I learned from the gentleman
who made leather goods below that there had been out-of-control
rages and that all my things had been thrown out of the window. The
police had been called to keep the peace. Mr X made the excuse that I
had made him do it by not coming home. What was happening? I was
trapped in a progressively ever more horrible relationship. I made
the decision to leave. At the earliest opportunity, I slipped out to
make a reverse-charge call to my mother – Mr X made sure I had no
cash – and asked her if she could arrange a pre-paid ticket for me to
await collection at the Air France desk at Nice airport, so that I could
just pick it up when I got there and go straight to the gate. I took a bus
to the airport, but when I got there, Mr X was waiting for me. I was
plunged into gloom and despair. I felt totally trapped as he begged,
and presented his excuses, and tried to explain himself. I gave in yet
again and went back, all the while asking myself what was I alive for?

PG:
The awfulness was escalating. What next?

JK:
Within a week, he had got into another rage and locked me out. I
went for a walk around the citadel. At one point, holding back the
tears, I sat on a bench wondering how to get out of this situation.

Suddenly someone grabbed me from behind and, before I could think, someone else grabbed my ankles. I was literally carried into the undergrowth, powerless despite my struggles. A hand over my mouth and a knife at my throat, my clothes were ripped, my jeans pulled off and, heart thumping, I was raped, not just by one but by both men. It was terrifying and I had no way to stop the assault. Afterwards, I was left like a used rag to hobble home. Home? This surely wouldn't have happened were it not for the fact that I had an insane husband. I had to wait until I was more composed; then I went back, said I was sorry, and had a bath. But why should I be saying sorry? Nothing made sense any more under the constant pressure of this man's scary, crazy behaviour.

Home was now a prison, with a guard. My instinct was to try and predict the rages, but this couldn't save me. After yet another tirade of insults and withering words, I was shoved out of the door in a poisonous gust of verbal abuse. I was in an earthquake of strangled emotions. I acknowledged to myself that I couldn't keep going. I was crumbling; anything was better than this. It seemed to me that the only way out was if I disappeared for good, that death was the only option. I had been very scared the day before when, with a kitchen knife in his hand, he had cornered me, his face black, contorted with anger. I could see it on a newspaper headline, 'Young woman found dead in Saint-Tropez – husband suspected'. Well, I went to three pharmacies, in each of which Mr X bought painkillers and sleeping pills, explaining that he wasn't well and needed more. I made the rounds, collecting the pills, then swallowed them all, walked down to the cemetery and sat on the high wall, which had a long drop down to the sea and rocks below. No one was about. I felt calm and still, listening to the waves. The sea breeze kissed my face. I waited for …. I have no memory of when I fell. Consciousness returned several hours later. By now, the sky was black. I wasn't dead, but I felt numb and thick, and my brain was hardly working. Was it some deep-rooted will to live that made me crawl off the rocks and up the steep cliff edge to the top? It didn't feel like it was me making this choice. I was wet, not drowned; my head and face felt sticky. I was dulled. I couldn't stand. I crawled on all fours, down the street, past my sweet friends' house. Everyone was asleep in the October night. I arrived at the door of our apartment and rang the doorbell, returning to hell – I've no idea why. Then darkness once again. I awoke in an ambulance and gradually became aware of the hustle and bustle of a hospital, with gentle voices and gentle hands. I let go, and let sleep and care embrace me.

With fifteen stitches in the gash in my head, many abrasions, and two broken ribs, I was kept in the hospital for three days. I refused the visitor. Someone came to try and discover what had happened, but I didn't open up. An overwhelming emotion of shame engulfed me. Shame that maybe I was so worthless that another person could treat me this way. Processing my thoughts, I eventually chose the path of escape. Unlike previous episodes, I knew that this time it had to be carefully planned. Mr X now kept my passport under lock and key. He took back any change after I had been shopping, so controlling was he. It took about a month of careful arranging and I depended on the trust of three people. The lovely girl at the pizzeria said that I had a bed whenever I needed it. The old man upstairs told me that he would give me 100 francs to get me to the airport. My mother, again in a reverse-charge call, confirmed that the pre-paid ticket was still with Air France. I was quiet and calm. I had made the decision.

Of course there was another bout of anger and drinking, which went over one day and into the next. So, leaving him in a comatose sleep, I took my passport from the cupboard that fortunately he hadn't locked, tucked it in the back of my jeans and quietly let myself out, heart pounding. I crept upstairs and the old man gave me the 100-franc note. I went to the pizzeria and told my friend that I had left. 'Good', she said and took me to her flat. I knew that I couldn't be found here. I rested up. I was doing all this with great clarity. At dawn, I was on the first bus out; then I got the train to Nice. At the airport, sure enough, my ticket was waiting. I went through customs as soon as I could, keeping an eye out. With my heart beating fit to burst, I boarded the plane. I settled into my seat and was amazed that here I was, ready for take-off. Suddenly, over the intercom I heard 'There is a message for Miss Jill Kennington.' I thought, 'My God, has he come to the airport?' I stayed silent, but a few minutes later, a stewardess came up to me and said there is an urgent phone call. I told her the simple truth, that I was leaving my husband and that I was not talking to him. This was accepted and we took off. Once we had landed and cleared customs, I called my mother and told her that I would get the bus to Oxford, which I did, and she and my stepfather – his name was Dr Stephen Hall – picked me up. Exhaustion took over when we arrived home. A beautiful warm bedroom awaited. I curled up and slept, and slept.

Finding freedom

*solace in the Hebrides – a relationship terminated –
new relationships begun – discovering an inner strength –
the joys of motherhood –a burden is finally lifted –
a tale of survival and forgiveness*

PG:
*Jill, I find it hard to imagine the turmoil you went through. How did you
pull yourself back together after all this?*

JK:
I collected myself over the next couple of weeks, in the safety of
my mother and stepfather's home, a fourteenth-century gatehouse,
which had a moat around it and lovely gardens and shrubs, created
by my mother. How appropriate that I should be in a fortified
gatehouse, which looked like a miniature castle, at once solid and
cosy, with a fire always burning. I slept in the turret room. Friends
next door lent me a bicycle, so I could reach them speedily in the
event of an intimidating visitor. Telephone threats came through all
the time, with abuse hurled at my mother. I visited David and Sandy,
who were in London, and they put me in touch with a solicitor and
with a specialist divorce lawyer. Things were immediately put into
action and papers were served on Mr X. He was now in Oxford, where
he had checked into a hotel. It felt far too close. If the phone rang
and it was him, I just hung up. He was furious that the grounds cited
were cruelty. A trip to North Uist, in the Outer Hebrides, to stay in my
mother's crofter cottage, was a healing experience – beauty and space
by day and a snug peat fire by night. Two of my dearest friends came
over for a few days, which was a reminder of the specialness of true
friendship. I was divorced within four months. I could make a clean
start. Not only had I just turned forty in January, I had also turned the
page to a new chapter. Little was I to know that the next year I would
remarry.

But every step has a meaning and, before meeting my future husband,
I had a significant love affair. One evening, in my friend Juliet's cosy
cottage in Gloucestershire, with my gorgeous friends and a couple
of their friends, we had supper by the fire. We played music and
talked. One of the friends was a musician who played the guitar. He
was a beautiful artist and actor. A week or so later, there was a mutual
realisation of the magnetic attraction between us. There followed a
quiet and gentle love affair. It was as if I was being fed for the first

time in a very long time. Playing tracks by John Williams and Joan Armatrading, my senses came alive. Sunshine coursed through my veins; my nerve endings awoke; it was an amazing gift. It was to be short but incredible; I regained confidence and felt fulfilled. As with an earthquake, there is devastation but the cracks in time will reveal new growth. I had come up for air. Vulnerability with honesty is beautiful. So I was ready for life and ready to grow, confident at last of an inner strength and resources. And then I met and very soon married the man with whom I was to share thirty-plus years. His name is Richard. When I met Richie, as he is known to family and friends, a part of me was very much in need of stability after all the emotional upheavals of the previous years. Richie seemed to provide this lifeline, but I also knew that he had his own demons and that things might not always be plain sailing. Shelving any such concerns, I was ready to take the plunge. I had the sense that he would be the father of my future children. He already had two marvellous children from his first marriage, Jamie and Chloë, who spent many weekends with us and always came to the annual Cornish holiday at Medla, the family house overlooking the beach at New Polzeath.

We got off to a good start. My new, more settled life certainly had its rewards. I particularly valued the gathering up of friendships, rekindled after fifteen years. This was extremely special. Most special of all though was the fact that, thanks to my being healthy, plus a huge dollop of luck, I became pregnant at the age of forty-one. The birth of my first daughter, Charlotte, felt like a miracle, crowned three years later by the birth of my second daughter, Christabel. I felt so blessed.

Then, one day, I came home in my little Fiat after a shopping trip, with Charlotte in a basket, drove up to our London home, Dalmeny House, near the Victoria and Albert Museum, and nearly had a heart attack. A figure was inspecting the bells. It was Mr X. I kept moving, driving round the block, returning after half an hour, when the coast was clear. Mr X was stalking me. I learned that he had questioned the nearby fruit and vegetable stallholder many times, trying to find out about me. The porter at Dalmeny House had to stop him coming into the building. Then there was a spate of phone calls. I always said, 'I have a new life now. I am happy', and put the phone down. Although now I only did the occasional fashion shoot, or made the occasional contribution to a documentary, Mr X always found out and rang up, either with praise or criticism. I always put the phone down and never asked him a question. When we first moved to the country, he would call up to say that he would always know where I was. I didn't want to be spooked, believing that good always overcomes bad; however, I wasn't comfortable about the knowledge he had of everything I did.

Jill's portrait of her daughters Charlotte and Christabel, 1990

Exhibitions, articles, or a fashion shoot provoked a reaction. I needed to be careful. But now I felt better able to keep it in perspective. Family life was helping keep me grounded.

PG:

You had certainly earned the right to enjoy this new chapter of your life. And you eventually settled in the country?

JK:

Before our relatively recent move to Dorset, we had lived for a number of years in a magic place in Sussex called Entry Hill. It needed a lot of care and work, but whatever efforts went into it, I, in particular, reaped a tenfold reward. Having been brought up on a farm, I loved living in the country. We had only just moved in; we had been there for barely twenty-four hours, and the girls and I were doing art round the dining-room table, when the phone rang. It was Mr X. I was really angry at this intrusion and told him bluntly to fuck off and never call again. My girls looked shocked, as I normally didn't get angry, and asked, 'Who was that?' I told them it was my difficult ex-husband and that was that. This prompted me to have this gorgeous creative home blessed by the vicar. He came round a few days later, blessed each room and each of us. It felt very important to do this. For a while, I was aware of the size of the garden, all the woods and the stream, and the thought troubled me that our isolation in this landscape left us vulnerable if someone wished to make trouble. But after this comforting gesture, I let go of my anxieties. That was indeed the last call I ever had from Mr X. Perhaps my genuine display of anger worked.

Then one day, before our move to Dorset, Mr X's sister-in-law called out of the blue and said, 'Please can we talk?' I had met her only twice in fifteen years, with Mr X's brother and mother. Ours was a non-relationship. I was taken by surprise as she quickly said, 'Please don't put the phone down', and proceeded to explain that Mr X was very ill and was asking if I would go and see him. I explained, in a nutshell, that he had given me a hellish time for so many of our years together, and beyond, and I wouldn't go. For some inexplicable reason, I added, 'unless he is on his deathbed and won't be getting better.' She also added that he had been a terrible brother to her husband and had literally arrived on their doorstep with nothing, asking for help. That seemed like the end of the matter, but a few months later a nephew called; he introduced himself and told me that the time had arrived and Mr X wouldn't last the week. Two days later, I drove to the nephew's house two hours away. He was a very kind man. We talked and he totally understood my position. So we then drove in tandem to the hospital, went up in the lift, then sat for a while as I took the time to calm my angst and fear. Completely composed and knowing what I had to do, I slowly pushed the door open.

My nostrils filled with that hospital smell. I thought, 'I fear no evil.' A kindly looking male nurse invited me in and offered me a chair by the bed. I said gently that I would only be a moment and that I preferred to stand. I looked towards the bed. He had shrunk. My thoughts were, 'How could I ever have been scared of this insignificant body in this bed?' One of the last times he had hit me, I recalled, was on the back of my head, so hard that it floored me and there was a fizzing, paralysing sensation for a while. Yet here I was, strong and confident. His eyes were closed. I took a deep breath and said, 'Hello … Jill here', at which point his eyes suddenly opened and he looked at me, then closed them again. This gave me something of a shock, so summoning up courage, I said, 'You were very cruel and gave me hell, but I forgive you.' Then I immediately left the room. The nephew was there in the corridor and at that point I let go and floods of involuntary tears flowed from my eyes, cleansing this bizarre situation. I said to the nephew, 'God grant me the serenity to accept the things I cannot change, the courage to change the things I can, and the wisdom to know the difference.' I had just put into practice the Serenity Prayer. I had found courage. He died a couple of weeks later and I realised that a persistent burden had finally been lifted from me. I was cleansed. I had been released. I had found true freedom.

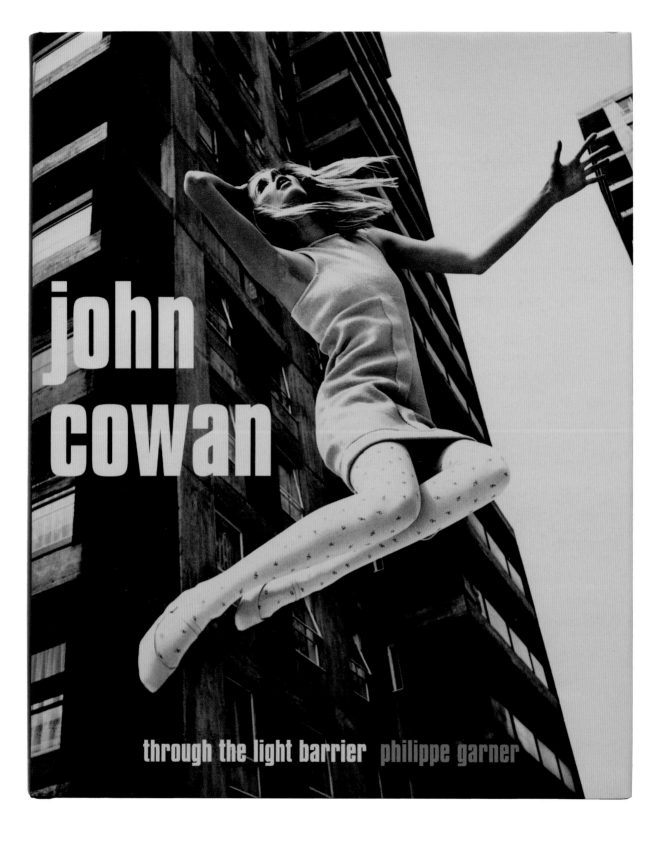

Philippe Garner, *John Cowan through the light barrier*, 1999

New chapters

the other side of the camera – portraits and landscapes –
looking back at the Sixties – a few encores – grounded in family life –
the roller-coaster of our lives

PG:

Jill, you have told your story with remarkable frankness. Thank you. But life
surely had new chapters in store after your modelling years.

JK:

My London-Paris-Rome modelling years seem like a lifetime ago.
They were extraordinary, exhilarating years. I am pleased to have
set down this record of those times. Life since then has brought me
surprise and variety – and my two gorgeous daughters have been
a great source of joy. Motherhood felt both totally natural and an
amazing privilege for me, and brought unexpected gifts. I understood
unconditional love. Meanwhile, before my re-marriage, I had bought
myself a camera, a classic 35mm Nikon. Having spent so many years
in front of a camera, I now wanted to make pictures for myself. My
first trip immediately after I bought the camera was to North Uist, in
Scotland. Then, still before I got re-married, I went with some good
friends to Bequia, in the Caribbean. That was terrific, and I took many
photographs of local people. I really loved the process of making
pictures. I began doing portraits informally, and soon found myself
being asked to make them. Landscapes, always a passion, became my
other favoured subject, both in Britain and, when the opportunity
arose, in other lands. I had travelled far and wide in my modelling
years – from the Middle East to North America, from the Arctic to the
deserts of Africa – and this gave me a lasting appetite for seeing the
world, its natural and man-made wonders. The urge to travel seems
to be in my blood.

I love black and white, and have remained faithful to film, working for
some years with a great printer, Bob Wiskin, who started in the *Vogue*
darkroom in the Sixties. I have had opportunities to exhibit my work,
at places such as the Chelsea Arts Club. The National Portrait Gallery
has a number of my pictures in their archive, which I am very happy
about. I enjoy the various occasions when I am invited to revisit my
early modelling years, sharing my story with new audiences and with
new generations who were not even born during those years. In 1991,
the Victoria and Albert Museum held the exhibition *Appearances*,
devoted to post-war fashion photography. I featured in several images
in the show and was asked to speak within a related lecture series. I

was not so keen on the idea of taking the stage alone, and suggested, rather, that I should be in conversation with someone, as I thought that would be an easier format for me than a formal lecture. You, Philippe, were asked to do this with me, and that is how we met, as you surely recall, and now we have a long history of collaboration, culminating in the present project to set down my memories on paper.

PG:

Yes, that V&A event brought us together. And, of course, set me off on my researches into John Cowan's life and career.

JK:

Yes, one thing led to another, including your 1999 book on John and the V&A exhibition that drew attention once again to his great work, which had been largely forgotten. It was so exciting to see those stunning pictures in the book and on the museum walls, and for my role in so many of them to be recognised. That exhibition introduced my daughters to their mum's previous life. And it has gone on, with pictures from my early career featuring in exhibitions in international art museums and with invitations to be present and sometimes to talk or be interviewed. It was wonderful to meet up again with Veruschka at the opening of your Photographers' Gallery exhibition on *Blow-Up*. That was in 2006. More recently, I have been invited to Vienna and to Amsterdam in the context of exhibitions relating to *Blow-Up* and to the Sixties, and in London to events in connection with the major exhibition on Mary Quant at the Victoria and Albert Museum.

Some time ago, I joined a new agency for older models and was pleased to do the occasional job. I was in *Harper's Bazaar*, and featured in a BBC television documentary about cosmetic surgery, expressing my firm belief that you cannot and should not deny the passage of time and that I personally would never have recourse to going under the knife. In recent years, I have also done several fashion shoots. One was a beauty campaign for Selfridges. It was titled 'Hello Beautiful', and was used on one of the huge billboards on the M4 coming into London. Fifty years ago I was on one of those self-same billboards for a BP ad shot by Donovan. I have also featured in a video ad for Rimmel, a shoot for the American clothing brand Anthropologie, and more recently a Benneton campaign as well as a multi-page feature in the Irish edition of *Tatler*. I am always so pleased to be able to share those aspects of my past that seem to be an abiding interest for people fascinated by the Sixties, and to stay a little bit involved in the world of fashion.

I have never stopped being grateful for what life has brought me through those decades centred on my family. That said, my marriage was not exactly the idyll I had hoped for. Richie could be so kind and big-hearted, but he was a fragile, troubled soul who needed careful managing, and particularly so through some very difficult periods. Life with someone else can be a roller-coaster of unexpected happenings, of which there have been many. A few years ago, Richie's beloved son Jamie died tragically, and this was followed by the premature death of his daughter Chloë, who had been through some very dark times. A catastrophic hole was left, yet we had no choice but to try and come to terms with it and learn how to keep going. Richie took these shocks very badly and his ability to cope with life going forward was dramatically undermined. These and other events are too recent and still too painful for me to feel ready or able to discuss in any detail. But the bitter reality was that, for a number of reasons, our marriage became untenable and divorce was the only way for me to survive emotionally intact.

I couldn't live happily without feeling close to nature. Perhaps this was instilled deep within me from my earliest years, brought up on that farm and so closely connected to the land, the animals, and the seasons. I need to feel the earth beneath my feet, and absorb its strength and peace. On crazy days, it is remarkably powerful; on soft days, it is gentle and nourishing. It is never the same, always changing, evolving. Travel has meant great family holidays, but also some memorable trips alone – to New Zealand, Nepal, and Namibia – which have been wonderful opportunities to experience awe-inspiring landscapes. And to take photographs. But friends and family are precious above all else, and my philosophy on life, humanity, and nature is constantly enriched by sharing and giving. I do have a thirst for life. You never know what may come next, what is round the corner.

Landscape near Beachy Head, Sussex, by Jill, 2004

Acknowledgements

The project to record and publish this memoir has been a long and rewarding one that would not have been possible without the generous help and support of a number of people. We take this opportunity to express our considerable gratitude to:

Vince Aletti, Alex Anthony, Martin Barnes, Penny Breia, Erica Creer, Richard Dawkins, Diana Donovan, Lucy Duckworth, Jason Elphick, Tony Fisher, Lucilla Garner, Christopher Gregory, Roger Hargreaves, Denny Hemming, Sanjay Kalideen, Conor and Michelle Meyer-Masterson, Gunilla Mitchell, David Montgomery, Walter Moser, the late Paddy Moyes, Robin Muir, Alistair O'Neill, Terence Pepper, the late Adam Smith, Stuart Smith, Helen Tory, and Harriet Wilson.

Jill Kennington and Philippe Garner

Cover: Jill, by Peter Rand, 1963
P. 2 Jill, by John Cowan, Sandwich Bay, November 1964
P. 4 Jill, by John Cowan, March 11th 1964
P. 6 Jill, contact sheet by Peter Rand, 1963
P. 8 Jill, by John Cowan, 1966

Published in 2021 by
Unicorn, an imprint of Unicorn Publishing Group
5 Newburgh Street
London
W1F 7RG
www.unicornpublishing.org

Text © Jill Kennington and Philippe Garner

Image sources: The illustrations in this volume are derived directly from original documents, including photographs, magazines, tear sheets, and newspaper cuttings. Those on pages 10, 12, 47, 114, 173, 191, and 198 are from the Jill Kennington archive; all the others are from the Philippe Garner archive.

Photographer credits: David Bailey (p. 59), Gian Paolo Barbieri (pp. 164, 167), Peter Beard (pp. 114, 118, 120), John Cowan (pp. 2-3, 4, 8, 33, 38, 41, 43, 47, 84, 87, 92, 96, 102-103, 106, 110, 113, 125, 194), Terence Donovan (pp. 29, 54, 57), Arthur Evans (pp. 134, 137), John French (p. 30), Phillip Jackson (p. 48), Jill Kennington (pp. 191, 198), William Klein (p. 75), Saul Leiter (p. 72), Lichfield (p. 51), Michael McKeown (p. 128), David Montgomery (131), Helmut Newton (pp. 76, 79, 81), Norman Parkinson (pp. 35, 88-89), Peter Rand (front cover, p. 6), Willy Rizzo (p. 151), Jeanloup Sieff (p. 61), Ronald Traeger (p. 142), unknown (pp. 10, 12).

The illustrations on pages 54, 59, 81, 96, 102-103, 110, 113, 142, 164, and 167 are reproduced courtesy of Condé Nast.

Designed by Stuart Smith

Printed by Fine Tone Ltd

ISBN 978-1-913491-92-5

10 9 8 7 6 5 4 3 2 1